CLASS-
PASSING

CLASS-PASSING

Social Mobility in Film and Popular Culture

Gwendolyn Audrey Foster

Southern Illinois University Press
Carbondale

    Library of Congress Cataloging-in-Publication Data
Foster, Gwendolyn Audrey.
   Class-passing : social mobility in film and popular
culture / Gwendolyn Audrey Foster.
       p. cm.
Includes bibliographical references and index.
   1. Mass media and culture—United States. 2. Social
mobility—United States. I. Title.
P94.65.U6F67 2005
305.5'13'0973—dc22   2005002318
ISBN 0-8093-2655-8 (cloth : alk. paper)
ISBN 0-8093-2656-6 (pbk. : alk. paper)

Printed on recycled paper. ♻

The paper used in this publication meets the minimum
requirements of American National Standard for
Information Sciences—Permanence of Paper for Printed
Library Materials, ANSI Z39.48-1992.∞

For Dana

CONTENTS

ACKNOWLEDGMENTS

No one writes a book alone, but in the creation of this text, I had considerable help from my friends and colleagues. My heartfelt thanks go to the reference librarians at the University of Nebraska's Don L. Love Library, who fielded many research inquiries during the writing of this manuscript. I thank the chair of the Department of English, Linda Ray Pratt, for her support and caring interest in this project and her support of film studies as a discipline within academe. I also thank the members of the UNL Research Council, who awarded me a grant to support me through the research of this book, which is deeply appreciated. My sincere thanks also go to Dean Richard Hoffmann, who granted me a faculty development leave in spring 2004 to write this book. The film and print archivists at the Museum of Modern Art Research Library assisted me with many research inquiries throughout the writing of this book, and I appreciate their patience and expertise. I must also thank the many writers who work in the area of class, from bell hooks to Stanley Aronowitz, for providing insights that illuminated new areas of inquiry for this text. Sincere thanks to Dana Miller, for her expert assistance in the preparation of this manuscript, and to Therese Myers, who did a superb job in the copyediting of the text. Most of all, I thank my partner in crime, my love, my life, my editor, my muse, Wheeler Winston Dixon, who is incredibly supportive of my work in all capacities. Without his support and guidance, this book never would have appeared.

CLASS-
PASSING

Class-Passing and the American Dream

We all class-pass. We all negotiate class. We all experience and perform class. Yet very little discussion of class occurs, very little attention is paid to class in popular culture and film. In this book, I consider the many ways in which we class-pass in contemporary popular culture, using TV reality shows, video games, advertisements, the Internet, and twenty-first-century digital cinema as some of the key media of access to this fantasy universe. As bell hooks writes in her groundbreaking study of class, *Where We Stand: Class Matters*, "as a nation we are afraid to have a dialogue about class even though the ever-widening gap between rich and poor has already set the stage for ongoing and sustained class warfare" (1). Indeed, hooks calls class "the uncool subject" (1), as opposed to race or gender and, I would add, sexuality. Another of the few who address class in popular culture is Yvonne Tasker, the author of *Working Girls: Gender and Sexuality in Popular Cinema*.

The repression of the discussion of class is itself a subject that should make us pause, because the repressed will always return and cause us to lurch and gasp and recognize desire. In his article "Is There a Class in This Text? The Repression of Class in Film and Cultural Studies," David James looks into the ways in which class has been marginalized in academic study of cinema. He notes how our field moved away from classical Marxism toward identity theory and, in particular, theory grounded in psychoanalysis.

In the 1970s we saw a radical shift toward the study of feminism, race, ethnicity, sexuality, and even disability, all revolving around identity markers such as gender and race and all thoroughly grounded in psychoanalysis. The problem I have with psychoanalysis, that it can only theorize an overdetermined sense of identity based on a history of desire that is itself based on lack, is a problem James identifies.

> The only social difference that film theory could thenceforth register was the specificity that psychoanalysis itself could theorize, that is sexual difference. After this point, given that even the historically specific family structure was not admissible as a mediating agency in the structuration of the unconscious and of language around the phallus or its lack, the main currents of cinema studies had no theoretical means of addressing issues of class. (195)

Similarly, Gilles Deleuze and Félix Guattari find psychoanalytical approaches truly lacking. Their call to action is *Anti-Oedipus: Capitalism and Schizophrenia,* a text published in 1977. Mark Seem, in his introduction to the book, stresses that Freud, Lacan, and others reduce the body to an oedipal neurotic figure. Seem explains that Deleuze and Guattari's work attacks "all reductive psychoanalytical and political analyses that remain caught within the sphere of totality and unity, *in order to free the multiplicity of desire from the deadly neurotic and Oedipal yoke*" (xx; emphasis mine). Deleuze and Guattari are obsessed with freeing desire from the standard psychoanalytic frameworks, which they see as colonizing imperialism at work. They insist that the oedipal framework has reinscribed desire within a capitalist framework—and a very limited one at that. Their point is that the unconscious, as it had been oedipalized, was reduced to an unconscious "that was capable of nothing but expressing itself—in myth, tragedy, dreams[, and that it] was substituted for the *productive unconscious*" (24; emphasis mine). I wish to resuscitate and borrow from Deleuze and Guattari's ideas primarily because I think that they provide a Marxist reclamation of desire from the overdetermined and reductionist couch of psychoanalysis. The idea of a *productive unconscious* seems to me to be a place where I can begin to understand the cinematic fixation with class mobility because it insists on the social negotiation of desire, moving desire off the couch and into the collective fantasies of the capitalist American Dream, including fantasies of upward mobility that are often enacted and performed on-screen. Because both capitalism and psychoanalysis are dependent on projections of lack, whether it is lack of a penis or lack of a job, "lack as a function of market economy is the art of a dominant class" (28). Indeed, Deleuze and Guattari insist that we move away from capitalist logic because it falsifies and maintains a split between social reality and private fantasy, where desire lives. Desire is social; so is production and so is fantasy, according to their thinking, and any split between "social production" and "desiring production" inscribes us into a system in which social mobility, or any desire for that matter, is impossible to conceive of or recognize.

> As long as we are content to establish a perfect parallel between money, gold, capital, and the capitalist triangle on the one hand, and the libido, the anus, the phallus, and the family triangle on the other, we are engaging in an enjoyable pastime, but the mechanisms of money remain totally unaffected by the anal projections of those who manipulate money. (28)

The productive unconscious is constantly expressing itself on-screen and in popular culture, especially with regard to questions of class, yet with the exception of a few academics working the field of cultural studies and sociology, few are prepared to comment on class performances and classed acts that appear right in front of our noses merely because the desire for class mobility seems as normative and opaque as the American Dream itself.

Class-passing and class mobility are not usually treated as behaviors or fantasies that spring from desire, whether it be the work of the unconscious of the individual or that of the collective unconscious. Class-passing simply has been normed so intrinsically that it no longer stands out, much like whiteness. Like whiteness, it has been dangerously adopted as a norm. Richard Dyer's *White* exposed the danger of not recognizing whiteness, noting the "assumption that white people are just people" and adding that white people are treated as "just human" and all others are "something else" (2). Dyer also notes that lower classes are marked by a lack of whiteness. In art and poetry, for example, he finds that working-class people are rendered darker than middle- or upper-class people (113). "Class as well as such criteria of proper whiteness as sanity and non-criminality are expressed in terms of degrees of translucence, with murkiness associated with poor, working-class and immigrant white subjects" (113).

In my own study of whiteness, *Performing Whiteness: Postmodern Re/ Constructions in the Cinema,* I drew from Dyer's work but injected a heavy profusion of ideas about performing the body from the work of

Judith Butler. In studying the performativity of whiteness, in insisting that much of what we call whiteness is actually performed, I came upon and identified repeated acts of class-passing. I noticed that so many American films are not just about properly performing whiteness but also about performing class. A significant number of films, often but not always romances, comedies, and Horatio Alger–type narratives, are about class mobility and what I called class-passing. This class-passing often involves marrying up, marrying down, and moving through social positions because of a change in job, marriage, or any number of plot contrivances. I began to obsess about this notion of class-passing and its relationship to the American Dream of social mobility. I began to wonder how class-passing is like and unlike passing in terms of race or gender. As I wrote in 2003,

> Class-passing is in some ways like race-passing, gender-passing, or straight/gay-passing, but class-passing, like whiteness, is not often noticed or examined. It is essentially viewed as normative behavior, especially in America, where one is expected to do as much class-passing as possible, regardless of one's race, gender, or economic circumstances. (102)

Because so much work has been done in the area of race- and gender-passing, I turn to studies of passing across race and gender for help in understanding class-passing. Kathleen Pfeiffer's *Race Passing and American Individualism* brought me back to some questions I have long held about class-passing. For example, in her introduction, Pfeiffer notes that passing for white "has long been viewed as an instance of racial self-hatred or disloyalty" (27). But, Pfeiffer wonders,

> Must the passers' embrace of the potential for success to which their white skin avails them be seen simply as their co-optation by a culture founded on "white" values? Must passing necessarily indicate a denial of "blackness," or racial self-hatred and nothing more? (2)

Furthermore, I wondered, why is class-passing so often celebrated rather than problematized or stigmatized? Perhaps the answer lay in Pfeiffer's factoring in of American individualism as a mass-produced fantasy, a "social production," and a "desiring production," to quote Deleuze and Guattari. Pfeiffer suggests that we reenvision the race-passer

> as a figure who values individualism, who may be idiosyncratic, self-determining, or inclined toward improvisation, [inviting] a much richer and more complex reading. Moreover, when we recognize that the passer often demonstrates ambivalence about whiteness as well as black-

ness, we avail ourselves of the passing figure's more complicated nuances. Understood in this light, passing offers a problematic but potentially legitimate expression of American individualism, one that resists segregation's one-drop logic and thereby undermines America's consciously constructed ideology of racial difference. (2)

Mary Bucholtz also wonders why the concept of gender-passing is embraced when race-passing is generally rejected.

Why is a concept that is considered invaluable for understanding certain social categories rejected as a way of understanding others? The answer can be found in the eagerness with which poststructural feminism has declared the end of identity and the destruction of social categories. This event has not been met with answering cheers from all quarters, a reticence that is due to the fact that the implosion of sexual categories authorized by queer theory has not yet been matched by the eradication of racial and ethnic categories. The subversive appeal of queer identities lies precisely in their ability to be disguised. Metaphors of theater, parody, and drag permeate postmodern feminist writing, with little recognition that disguises cannot be as easily assumed by members of social groups whose identities have been imposed rather than assumed or appropriated—namely, members of nonwhite racial and ethnic groups. The categorizing power of skin color, hair, and facial features remains a reality for most Americans of non-European background, a fact that is often overlooked by white poststructural feminists. Whereas gender theorists celebrate passing as an achievement, a transcendence of sexual difference, in ethnic studies the phenomenon is generally considered an evasion of racism, an escape that is available only to individuals who can successfully represent themselves as white. (352–53)

Nevertheless, many critics agree that passing reveals the constructedness of race and acts as a critique of race. Gayle Wald adds that race-passing is not just about individualism and opportunism but also about imagining and reimagining "home."

Insofar as it is possible to generalize about racial passing narratives . . . [they] are concerned with elucidating concepts of "home" in relation to social categories of race, class, gender, sexuality, and nationality. In particular, they represent the struggles of subjects to imagine a "home" that would not demand their subjugation to, or confinement within, the various defining discourses alternatively imposed and wielded by the dominant culture. (51)

Returning to Deleuze and Guattari, I note a parallel concern for freedom, freedom from colonizing frameworks of desire as they are enacted in academic work or as they are enacted in treatments of class. Looking across a wide spectrum of film and popular culture, we find socially inscribed desires for icons of social mobility in everything from film to "reality" television. In 2003 the Fox network premiered *Joe Millionaire,* a show in which a construction worker passed himself off as a millionaire to choose an appropriate "mate" from several women contestants. The desire to watch "Joe" pass reeled me in, along with 40 million others who tuned in for the finale (Prose 59). The idea of the class-passing white male figure intrigued me as much as the women's performances of class on the program. Another reality-based program that I found myself watching was *The Simple Life,* in which socialites Paris Hilton and Nicole Richie flaunt their privileged status in front of a working-class midwestern farm family. The show was wildly successful, and I wondered why.

Nobody won any money. The two young female stars did not pretend to be anything other than spoiled, pampered, and elite. They did not really "slum" as much as highlight class differences by their very presence. They provided a fantasy of contact between the classes, and that point of contact is explosive and meaningful to the average American. That point of contact is not unlike the hybrid space of the class-passer, the race-passer, or the transvestite. The hybridity of the point of contact between classes is a desire capitalist America produces and maintains. It was similarly exploited in such programs as *Who Wants to Marry a Millionaire?, Trading Spouses, Wife Swap, The Bachelorette,* and *My Big Fat Obnoxious Fiancé,* in which a young upper-middle-class woman tries to win a half million dollars by passing off an obnoxious and overweight actor, who pretends to have absolutely no class whatsoever, as her future husband. The shows are best watched by viewing the pilot episode, checking in once in a while, and waiting for the final episode, not just because the show is boring and repetitive but also because the finale reveals the class-passing and the class-passer, which is the only thing really worth watching in these programs. As Francine Prose writes, these programs reinscribe a rather conservative vision of the American Dream.

Observant readers may already have noted that the guiding principles to which I've alluded—flinty individualism, the vision of a zero-sum society in which no one can win unless someone else loses, the conviction that altruism and compassion are signs of folly and weakness, the exaltation of solitary striving above the illusory benefits of cooperative mutual aid, the belief that certain circumstances justify secrecy and deception, the invocation of a reviled common enemy to solidify group loyalty—are the exact same themes that underlie the rhetoric we have been hearing and continue to hear from the Republican congress and our current administration. (60)

The performers on so-called reality television shows perform a sort of minstrelsy that is in some ways reminiscent of blackface minstrelsy in performing class and rejecting the idea of a natural state of class even while they support the hegemonic desire for that natural or biological essence of class. As Kathleen Pfeiffer notes, "minstrelsy often reflected an anxiety regarding self-identity, a desire to define the self oppositionally," adding, "minstrelsy's genius was to be able to both display and reject the 'natural self'" (11). Thus, the point of contact, the rupture and fissure of class difference, is what lies at the heart of these "reality" programs. They are much like two race-passing films Gayle Wald discusses, Elia Kazan's *Pinky* (1949) and Alfred L. Werker's *Lost Boundaries* (1949), in that they "enable their protagonists to realize their American 'dreams' of professional success while also insisting that they remain in their 'places'" (87). But the difference is perhaps that the reality shows enable the audience to distance themselves from any painful reminder of their own class or race differences or anxieties.

Class-passing in "reality" programming both displays and disrupts the notion of class as an identity marker. Class-passing is certainly as problematic as race-passing, but both are also dependent on deception and American ideas about individualism and the worthiness of the American Dream. The tough thing in talking about class as a performative act is that real class differences, real consequences, real hardships, and real privileges that come with class certainly exist, just as real privileges and hardships exist with regard to real race-passing. I wish, however, to remain primarily in the realm of wishes, desires, and societal fantasies because they have to do with class, and I have a vested interest in talking about class and class-passing because I myself do not come from a background of class privilege.

I am struck by the ways in which even our language suggests that we rethink our notions of class and note that in many situations class is an act. Think of the term *class act* in a sentence such as, "She was such a class act." I can't think of a similar term that centers on another identity marker such as race, gender, or sexuality. Is it perhaps because *class* as a term refers to so many levels of signifiers? Class is not only about wealth, status, and birth but also about everyday performed behavior. How one does everything from eating to speaking to any kind of behavior is classed or troped by class. In this way, class trumps many other identity markers such as race, gender, or sexuality, does it not? If anyone can be a "class act," it stands to reason, then, that class, at least removed from actual, tangible real wealth or lack thereof, is all about performance and performativity.

Furthermore, class's essential performative nature allows one, offscreen or on-screen, to perform in several class levels at the same time. Class mobility is at the center of the American Dream, and performance punctuates that dream itself. Think of the language we use to indicate that one is moving up or down in class: from *slumming* to *putting on airs* to *high-hatting* to the black colloquial term *representing*. Perhaps the cinema and other popular culture arenas allow us to perform and enact movement across class and afford us a class-passing space where audiences can vicariously and safely experience a shared subjectivity with the class-passer. Our collective fantasies not only seemingly allow us a place of class mobility but also reinforce the idea that class is both mutable and rigid. Change is possible. Upward mobility is performed. Downward mobility is also possible and, in some cases, desirable.

The very nature of acting itself is about *passing;* passing oneself off as an/other and, in the process, throwing off the shackles of any natural or normed identity markers. The nature of being a spectator, similarly, is to be a sort of class-passer. A spectator is invited to coproduce the meaning of a text, and the spectator is allowed to identify equally with the faux bachelorette and with Paris Hilton. The nature of being a filmmaker or a storyteller seems invested in class-passing, too. A writer must "pass" off a story—"pass" off a narrative. Narratives are playful and involve pretending and, of course, believing in the viability of passing. All narratives offer sites for participants to negotiate passing through identification or other spectator positions.

The nature of the spectator is mobile, mutable, at one with the on-screen narratives, even multiple narratives, multiple performers. We all allow ourselves the class-passing opportunity to pretend we are, if for only a few fleeting moments, Fred Astaire and Ginger Rogers. Indeed in the very early days of silent film, movies taught class-passing through spectatorial involvement. Steven J. Ross argues in *Working-Class Hollywood* that "movies could teach immigrants what it meant to belong to a particular class" (21). One could easily argue that movies not only encouraged class-passing but also that spectatorship itself is a form of class mobility. Before movie distributors catered to the wealthier classes, they catered to the masses of lower-class and working-class people, many of them new immigrants. As Ross notes, movie watching easily became the pastime of working people, especially immigrants.

> Immigrants were especially drawn to an entertainment that required little knowledge of English. The Russian Jew, the German, the Austrian, or the Italian who has not been in this country a week and cannot understand English, explained one socialist daily, goes to the motion picture theaters because what he sees on the screen is very real to him, and he understands as well as the American. The widespread popularity of movies also helped break down long-standing patterns of ethnic isolation among immigrant groups. Walking into a nickelodeon along the Bowery in New York City, one was likely to see a diverse audience of Chinamen, Italians, and Yiddish people, the young and old, often entire families, crowded side by side. (21)

In 1910, for example, moviegoers could enjoy fare such as *How Hubby Got a Raise* or any number of films that featured working-class protagonists and films that reinforced the possibility of upward class mobility and the American Dream. Charlie Chaplin, for example, and Buster Keaton played the down-on-his-luck man-out-of-work. In their films, Chaplin and Keaton would take any job to impress the female lead. Much of the humor in these films comes from being able to identify with the on-screen plight of the hero. Many could identify with his unemployment, his hope for a better future, and his quest for the American Dream. Ross identifies numerous early films that center directly on working people and working-class lives. Early narrative films, such as *The Skyscrapers* (1906), *The Tunnel Workers* (1906), *A Child of the Ghetto* (1910), and *The Lily of the Tenements* (1911), deal with actual street life and the consequences of poverty and labor.

Mary Pickford's films almost always deal with the plight of a young, unmarried, working-class girl. Her misfortune, various situations, and her persona offered the female spectator an oppositional example of class experience. Class identities were still somewhat in flux in the United States, and silent American cinema offered plenty of Marxist critique along with escapist fare. Not until the 1920s and 1930s did studio heads turn away from liberalism when they decided to go after the expanding middle-class audiences and become "respectable." As Ross notes,

> Far from being the liberal institution it is depicted as today, Hollywood pushed the politics of American cinema in increasingly noncontroversial and anti-radical directions. Studio moguls realized they could make big money by turning moviegoing into a "respectable" entertainment that catered to the rapidly expanding and amorphous ranks of the middle class. (9)

Ross paints a fairly depressing picture of the politics of the newly developing studio system and its products. The disappearance of controversial films comes at the same time that society was changing in terms of class into the haves and have-nots.

> Hesitant to make controversial films that might alienate newly won audiences, studios abandoned old themes of class conflict in favor of making films that promoted conservative visions of class harmony; films that shifted attention away from the problems of the workplace and toward the pleasures of the new consumer society. (9)

Although studio heads could alter content and control themes, they could not alter the ability of spectators to desire to dream and to engage in all manner of spectatorial pleasures.

So much has been written about the exhilarating space of the movie palace as a place of primal or "primitive" spectatorial pleasure where fantasies could be lived out, but, Ross warns, "It was the *unpredictability* of these experiences that made moviegoing so appealing to the masses and so frightening to the elites" (15). With censorship, some say, movies emerged as class weapons. Many argue that the early days of cinema were geared far more toward proletariat audiences than toward wealthier ones. This generalization is true to a great degree; however, one must keep in mind that censorship often has unintended results. Perhaps by repressing straightforward depictions of class mobility and by problematizing class mobility, Hollywood fetishized it. It certainly could not hope to abandon the narrative of the American Dream. It could not possibly control audience reception, despite the many theories of the captive, unquestioning, passive, spectatorial voyeur.

In *Blue Collar Hollywood,* John Bodnar takes issue with Ross's arguments. Although Bodnar agrees with Ross about the change from early cinema to the cinema of the 1930s, Bodnar sees the later as more capable of providing myriad political themes and agendas.

> Ultimately the movies were—and still are—what Michel Foucault might call "heterotopias," or sites where many of the most powerful ideas in a culture could be represented at the same time. They merged attitudes that were rational and emotional, moral and immoral, angry and sentimental. A typical film story generally contained contrasting images of common people and tended to integrate numerous points of view. . . . (xviii)

Moviemakers could not afford to abandon wholesale the ideas found in popular culture and novels. A look across the cinematic landscape finds many narratives that center around class mobility.

One of the most obvious examples is Anthony Minghella's *The Talented Mr. Ripley* (1999), in which Matt Damon plays a penniless young man who accepts a job from an American millionaire to go to Europe and locate his son. Damon (as Ripley) ends up murdering the wealthy son, played by Jude Law, and for the better part of the film, we watch Damon attempt to class-pass. He must learn how to dress, how to treat those beneath his station, and how to deal with all the accoutrements of the aristocratic wastrel, as well as the girlfriend, the yacht, and the money. He is very good at what he does, and the audience can engage in spectatorial class-passing with him. Adapted from the Patricia Highsmith novel, the film itself is a remake of the French version from 1960, René Clément's *Purple Noon*, which starred Alain Delon and which was arguably a better adaptation of the assumed-identity thriller. Oddly enough, *The Talented Mr. Ripley* was to have starred Leonardo Di Caprio as Ripley; only later would Di Caprio play the lead role of a class-passer in Steven Spielberg's *Catch Me If You Can* (2003). In *Catch Me If You Can*, Di Caprio plays a con man, actually a very young con man based on a real-life figure, Frank Abagnale Jr., who passed himself off as an airplane pilot, a doctor, and a lawyer. His class-passing is seen as a pathetic call for help and parental guidance, and he befriends his own captor, the FBI agent played by Tom Hanks.

Hanks played a variant of the class-passing figure in 1988 in director Penny Marshall's *Big*, in which a young boy wishes to be grown up and he magically becomes a young executive for a toy company. Hanks's character not only experiences the challenge of passing himself off as a boy in a thirty-year-old man's body but also demonstrates that age is a form of class, or at least it can be a form of class. As a "man," the boy must learn the middle-class ways of dressing, shaving, eating, and, of course, courting women. His girlfriend, played by Elizabeth Perkins, is constantly inspecting his performance; it isn't that she thinks he's a boy, it's more that she wonders whether he has any "class," any sort of upbringing that could explain his bizarre behavior.

How to behave in a manner in keeping with one's class is a central motif in much American cinema and popular culture. One ripe example is the Andy Hardy series of films produced between 1937 and 1958, all starring Mickey Rooney. In *Andy Hardy Meets Debutante* (George B. Seitz, 1940), Andy falls for a young woman above his social standing. Andy becomes a bit too full of himself in *Andy Hardy's Private Secretary* (Seitz, 1941). After graduating from high school, the working-class Andy hires a social secretary. He is smitten with a girl of a different class. He's not punished in the film, but the laughs are at his expense. Anne Shirley plays a young girl who class-passes upwardly in *Anne of Green Gables* (George Nicholls Jr., 1934). This film, which is an adaptation of L. M. Montgomery's book of the same name, revolves around the class mobility of a plucky young orphan who manages to persuade an older couple of means to take her in.

Inheriting money can sometimes mean trouble, as it does in *The Aristocats* (Wolfgang Reitherman, 1970). In this animated film, a cat and her offspring inherit a fortune, only to become the enemy of the scheming butler who can inherit the cash if he manages to get rid of the cats. Ida Lupino pretends to be a socialite in Raoul Walsh's *Artists and Models* (1937) only to have the other members of the cast, which includes Jack Benny, Gail Patrick, and Martha Raye, see through her. Rodney Dangerfield wreaks havoc with our notions of class and class mobility in *Back to School* (Alan Metter, 1986). Dangerfield plays a self-made millionaire who has no class, even though he is rich. He enrolls in college to encourage his son to complete his education and thus have the opportunities that he himself has been denied.

Being There (Hal Ashby, 1979) is another film that plays with class and passing in original ways. Peter Sellers plays an ordinary, perhaps mentally challenged gardener who is mistaken for a politically savvy genius and propelled into the presidency by his perceived "class," which is really only a series of pithy statements he picks up from watching television. Shirley MacLaine is hysterically funny as his love interest, who mistakes his lack of class, education, and quiet nature for genius and upper-class behavior.

My Blue Heaven (Herbert Ross, 1990) is another comedy that scrutinizes class through its bizarre plot and performances. Steve Martin plays a gangster in the FBI's witness protection plan who moves to the suburbs but cannot quite effectively class-pass. Martin's behavior as a crass, obnoxious, yet lovable gangster is campy and over the top. The upper class is construed as boring, whereas the working class is embraced as earthy and lovable.

Far from abandoning scenes of class conflict, Hollywood obviously embraces narratives of class conflict and emphatically produces conflicting messages about opportunities for class mobility. We are taught to do whatever is necessary to achieve upward class mobility on the one hand, while we are frequently discouraged from moving, dating, or marrying out of our class on the other. "Stick to your own kind," a line from Stephen Sondheim's lyrics for *West Side Story* (both the play and the film), is a central subtext of many texts in pop culture as well as literature.

At the same time, we repeat the Horatio Alger mythos wherein anyone in the United States can rise in class merely by pulling himself up by his bootstraps. Stay in your own class. Marry in your own class. Run away from your own class. Be happy with what you have. Make the most of it. Just do it. Go for it. But far from being a dangerous set of mixed signals, these seemingly schizophrenic messages not only satisfy our need to cling to the American Dream but also cause anxiety and desire for a fetishized class mobility.

An interesting example of our schizophrenic attitude toward class mobility comes in a popular advice manual from 1914 called *Pep: A Book of Hows Not Whys for Physical and Mental Efficiency. Pep*, as author Colonel William C. Hunter defines it, stands for poise, efficiency, and peace. The book is a fascinating look at the fabric that holds together the American Dream. It is a how-to manual that encourages upward class mobility through a change in attitude and physical fitness. It speaks to the worker in the modernist age in which everything supposedly moves faster, in which he or she is expected to be a machine just to keep up, not to mention move up the corporate ladder.

> Today the world looks at the future with fear and uncertainty because civilization is becoming complex, requirements of man more grasping. The great multitude is wrestling with mammoth problems, of labor, prohibition, taxes, cost of living, morality, white slavery, neurasthenia, worry, and the task of providing for a rainy day. On top of this, the

selfish purpose of nearly every man is to build a monumental fortune. The cry is ever on, on, ON! The rhythm caused by the intoxication of man's mental carburetor, pulsates the words go, go, GO! (14)

Throughout the book, Hunter advocates the same sort of advice dispensed these days by the likes of Dr. Phil and Dr. Laura. All it takes, after all, is "pep." "Success," he writes, "will not be handed to you in a pretty blue box, tied with silk ribbons" (83). The book has a wonderfully hypnotic tone that is rife with phrases such as, "You are going to have faith, not fear. You are going to say 'I will' instead of 'I can't'" (92). Other cultures may find slightly odd the slew of mixed messages throughout manuals such as *Pep*. On the one hand, the American Dream is achievable: "Forget your pedigree, throw aside your family pride. You must fight alone for your place" (83). On the other hand, we should waste not time envying the wealthy: "The duck should be proud of its ability to swim. The duck that envies the stork his long legs is a pessimist; the duck that glories in its superior swimming powers is the optimist" (93). Like so many movies, the colonel takes pains to remind us that millionaires are usually unhappy anyway. Under the subheading "Millionaires Seldom Smile" is a section that conflates the ideologies of Marxism and socialism.

I should like you to notice the faces of the next few millionaires you meet. I will give you a reward of a hard-boiled egg for every smile you can detect on millionaires' faces. As material possessions increase, worries increase and smiles decrease. Money-making is a foolish ambition if you really want happiness. You can be rich by saving your pennies, turning them into dollars and hoarding them away, and while you are doing this, your heirs are counting the days until you die and leave your fortune for them to squander. (95)

Such a passage would be riotously funny were it not for the fact that its subtext is so confusedly against social mobility, which is one of the main goals that the colonel sets out to help the reader pursue. Next, Hunter trots out the many pithy messages about the "downside" of being filthy rich because money cannot buy everything, as we all know, because the maxim has been drummed into our heads since we were children. The colonel even suggests that the upper classes suffer because of their class status. They are jealous of us, and this is a message strewn so emphatically through film and popular culture that it is as identifiable and prevalent as the portraits of Chairman Mao during his tenure. Here is a sample of the colonel's salve to those who are not rich:

Money will get many things for you. It is a present help in time of sickness, but money as a means to happiness is a forlorn hope.

The rich man you envy is looking at you, envying your health and contentment. While you envy his gold and bonds and jewelry and automobiles, he is envying your energy and strength and courage and health. And these treasures are far beyond the ability of dollars to purchase. (95)

Here we have the nuggets from the author that attempt to put the worker above the aristocrat as he is found in such nauseatingly compromised films as *It's a Wonderful Life*, Frank Capra's 1946 box-office failure that has nevertheless gone on to become "the" Christmas movie. As we all know, it's a sentimental tale about a failed working-class fellow, played by James Stewart, who is ultimately, improbably saved by helpful townfolk and guardian angels. After the film fell into the public domain, it became a classic that today is shown repeatedly during the Christmas season.

The film's success is unparalleled. In an age when very few people will even watch a black-and-white film, this one is trotted out as "the" classic tale, "the" narrative of the Christian American Dream. Now you can purchase expensive cheap plastic miniature replicas of the buildings, including the bank, of the town of Bedford Falls. Watch as your dwindling bank account reflects your fetishism of the tale of American compromise. As Steven J. Ross observes, "Frank Capra's populist fantasies may have made viewers feel good, but they proposed solutions that had little chance of succeeding offscreen" (244). Capra's films, such as *Mr. Smith Goes to Washington* (1939) and *Mr. Deeds Goes to Town* (1936), appear to be socially aware—yet they ultimately called for class stability and worked (and continue to work) against class mobility and ultimately against the American Dream, unless of course the American Dream is really not a matter of embracing a rise in class.

John Bodnar's *Blue Collar Hollywood* includes an extensive section on the politics of Capra films. Bodnar hints at the fascism I find at the core of Capra.

In Capra films, "the people" remained a mass of reasonably good citizens who could be led in a number of political directions. For him the path to a more democratic community was ultimately not in the hands of common people themselves but in the hands of the right kind of leader. (38)

Although Capra was raised in poverty, he "harbored a deep suspicion of Democratic reformers" and "he may have developed a feeling of contempt over time for his ethnic heritage and for those among the lowborn who had failed to pull themselves out of poverty as he had" (Bodnar 37). Capra films perfectly exemplify the working classes' contempt for themselves and perhaps explain why so many working-class people vote for leaders and support systems that hold them down and suppress class mobility. It is a warm and cozy sort of embrace of fascism. Although Capra "seldom failed to point out the faults of capitalism," his "politics were the quintessential politics of American mass culture" and his films were "imprecise speculations that seeped over and around conventional boundaries of class and gender rather than explicit polemics designed to serve the upper or lower classes," concludes Bodnar (36).

The schizophrenic politics of Capra films can be seen through decades of American cinema in films such as the leaden but politically interesting remake of *Cheaper by the Dozen* (Shawn Levy, 2003), the motto or tagline of which ought to be "Don't even think of being upwardly mobile," or "Huge family more important than your dreams, Mom and Dad." This problematic film stars the otherwise wonderful Steve Martin as Tom Baker, a dad who dreams of being a big-time football coach. His wife, Kate, played by Bonnie Hunt, has always wanted to pursue her writing career, which she gave up to become a stay-at-home mom for twelve kids. The children themselves are utterly selfish and without charm. They move from their version of Bedford Falls when dad obtains his dream job as coach of his alma mater's football team. Mom's book is published, and she is guilt-torn when asked to go on a book tour. The comedy is supposed to kick in when Dad tries to play Mom, and predictably, chaos ensues. In their big, new expensive home, a massive set that Nina Ruscio and Scott Meehan designed, the kids prove lousy at class-passing. They are invited to a party by their upper-crust neighbors, where they show the overly pampered kid across the street how to have a good time, working-class style. Everything rapidly falls apart and the family moves back to their crowded, unkempt, but happy house when Dad and Mom agree that their dreams are not worth more than their supposedly cuddly family. The film not only preaches against individualism and against pursuing the American Dream but also is profuse with other dangerous messages. For example, one of the reasons Tom Baker takes his dream job is that the college, as his employer, would provide free tuition for his twelve children. When he gives up this job, the narrative conveniently drops this important detail. Furthermore, the film preaches poor decision-making based on sentiment rather than rational problem solving.

As I watched the movie, I pictured Suze Orman, a popular television commonsense financial adviser screaming at Mom something such as, "Don't give up your dream of being a wildly successful author because you can't always be with your kids. Hire a babysitter! After all, the biggest and best present you can give your kids is financial solvency. What's the matter with this picture?" Dad gives up a job that offers free tuition to all of his children and Mom gives up a financially and emotionally rewarding career to sacrifice for the children, when in actuality they are not only acting as poor role models but also giving away their children's future. The actual tagline of the film is "This Christmas, the More . . . the Scarier!" and, yes, that people are being indoctrinated into making stupid financial decisions is truly scary. Apparently one loses one's ability to reason when one has twelve children, which brings us to the question of why they actually have twelve children in the first place. Family planning? Not for this family. The Bakers are truly a scary family, and *Cheaper by the Dozen,* the remake, has truly scary messages, especially considering that its politics are so different from the original, made in 1950 and directed by Walter Lang. The original *Cheaper by the Dozen* mixes a healthy dose of capitalism with two parts socialism, which may be a bit surprising for 1950, but then again maybe we are now in an age that is more like the 1950s than the actual 1950s.

In Lang's original version of *Cheaper by the Dozen,* Clifton Webb is an efficiency expert married to Myrna Loy. His book and his methods are used to raise the Gilbreth children. In the 1950 version, Dad dies at the end of the film, and Mom and children band together into a practically socialist effort to survive and eventually succeed at achieving the American Dream. That most people going to see the remake have no knowledge of the original, which is based on a Gilbreth-Carey novel, is worrisome indeed.

Could the miserable economy of the new millennium have compelled the rewrite folks to come up with a film that completely obliterates the ideology of the original? Are we seeing a return to Capraesque film ideology that seeks to pacify the masses who live in a world where actually achieving the American Dream is increasingly more difficult? I wonder. Only seven years earlier, in 1996, we were treated to a populist comedy that used Adam Sandler to promote the ideology of the American Dream. In *Happy Gilmore* (Dennis Dugan, 1996), Sandler plays a rejected hockey player who uses his skills on the golf course to save his grandmother's house. Sandler often plays a working-class guy in his comedies. The difference in ideology between *Cheaper by the Dozen* and *Happy Gilmore* are those very interesting differences between films that teach us to be financially stupid and those that teach us that upward mobility is not only possible but also a positive character development. Indeed, Sandler has made a career out of playing the romantic underdog who eventually wins the day through either sheer luck or his own machinations, as in his remake of Frank Capra's *Mr. Deeds Goes to Town,* which he revisualized as *Mr. Deeds* (Steven Brill, 2002).

We really do not know whether to demonize millionaires or to worship them. Thus we have confusing efforts such as Michael Schultz's *Disorderlies* (1987), which both demonizes and worships a Palm Beach millionaire played by Ralph Bellamy. This poor little millionaire's nephew, played by Tony Geary, is about to murder him, but to the rescue come none other than the Fat Boys, the black rap version of the Three Stooges. At first the film demonizes the millionaire, who initially looks down on the Fat Boys and their uncouth, downwardly mobile ways. But Ralph Bellamy's character is softened in contrast with his evil valet and his murderous nephew. The working-class boys come to the rescue here, and suddenly Bellamy is a sweet little old millionaire worth rescuing.

Capitalism and the American Dream do not come with a manual, and understanding the messages about just how to deal with the Otherness of wealth and privilege and its Other, the millionaire, is difficult. With such mixed messages, is it any wonder that we fetishize the millionaire as Other? Television is undergoing a fascinating switch, as rich becomes the new gay, in reality programs such as *The Simple Life, The Apprentice, Joe Millionaire, Boy Meets Boy, The Bachelorette,* and *The Littlest Groom.*

One thing these programs have in common is their set design and their unusual fixation with the accoutrements we associate with frivolous wealth: hot tubs, champagne, huge mansions, marble floors, designer gowns, butlers, and "hosts" who usually have either a British or an Australian accent. This fetishism of wealth and its accoutrements is not usually commented on. Reviewers and audiences mainly talk about the questionable morality of choosing a mate from a group of contestants," marrying on television, producers lying to contestants, and contestants lying to their friends, family members, and other contestants.

All of these things are indeed questionable, but we should not miss an opportunity to comment on the fetish cabinet of current reality programming, whether it be the limousine of Donald Trump or the body of Donald Trump, who appears in *The Apprentice,* a slapdash affair that pits contestants against one another in a cutthroat competition. Each week they try not to get fired by Mr. Trump. The program is mind-numbingly boring but trades in the possibility of mobility, the point of contact, the fissure of class mobility. It is surrounded by fixtures we associate with an aristocratic class that hardly exists anymore, a class that surrounds itself with butlers, fine cutlery, and, above all, tuxedos, as well as the masquerade and mimicry of wealth and privilege. *The Littlest Groom* features a small person who has to choose a mate from a pool of several young women, some of them tall, some small. The interesting thing is that we learn so little about the "star" and the women. They go out on "dates" that include fetishized images of limousines, private jets, waterfalls, gondolas, gazebos, and rings on velvet, as well as the makeup, hairdo, tuxedos, and elaborate dresses now fetishized in a weirdly populist fashion. These images conjure up filthy-richness and are interspersed with the thinnest of plots. A thread of a narrative barely exists. Whom will he choose? Will he choose a normal-size woman or a "dwarf"?

The real narrative in the reality program is the reaction shot. The reaction shot is more important than the master shot, even the shot of the exterior of the obscenely huge mansions rented for the shooting of these shows. The editing is masterfully bound to the reaction shot: shots of the women when they are "chosen," shots when they are "passed over"; either way reaction shots rule. The last episode of *My Big Fat Obnoxious Fiancé* was a veritable montage of reaction shots.

In fact, the oft-repeated promo for *My Big Fat Obnoxious Fiancé* included a carefully and brilliantly edited series of shots designed to lie to the audience. In this program, the "stars," the bride and groom, are planning a bogus wedding. To win the $1 million, they have to convince the bride's family that the wedding is not a sham. The final episode revolves around the suspense over whether the bride's family will object to the wedding at the altar. In the end, no one objects, but in the promo, the clever recutting of images suggests that members of the bride's family do indeed object and walk out. The essentiality of the reaction shot is what reality television needs to complete its imagistic circuit, as a mediating tool between the revisualized world and its ostensible audience.

In *Joe Millionaire,* the camera lingers on reaction shots in equal proportion to its ritual display of the objects associated with wealth and privilege. When Joe is in the hot tub with several women, the audience is treated to several repeated images of reaction shots of the women not invited into the hot tub, as well as reaction shots of Joe himself. *The Simple Life* is made up almost entirely of reaction shots and "reveal" shots with appropriate sound effects added in postproduction. We see myriad reactions of small-town Midwesterners to the quirky behavior of Paris Hilton and Nicole Richie, often accompanied by musical motifs ripped from the score of the classic television sitcom *Green Acres. The Simple Life* trades in fetishized images of not only millionaires' bodies and things but also Othered middle-class life. The camera lingers on the deep fryer when Ms. Richie makes onion rings in one episode. In another, we see endless shots of cows' behinds when the young women are asked to do farm chores. It is equal-opportunity fetishism from both sides, and it is all about the class system in the United States. The women of *The Simple Life* objectify the working (and out-of-work) people around them. They treat the young farmhands as studs and call them "hot." They dub one young boy "Chops" for his huge, beautiful smile. The Othering of the upper class as well as the lower and middle classes should make us pause. Francine Prose calls reality television a "Darwinian free-for-all" (64) and laments,

> If the lesson of reality TV is that anyone will do anything for money, that every human interaction necessarily involves the swift, calculated formation and dissolution of dishonest, amoral alliances, it seems naive to be appalled by the fact that our government has been robbing us to pay off its supporters in the pharmaceutical industry and among the corporations profiting from the rebuilding of Iraq. After you've seen a "real person" lie about his grandmother's death, you may be slightly less shocked to learn that our leaders failed to come clean about the weapons of mass destruction. (64)

These programs parody democracy, as Prose claims, and in the process they inevitably draw on the specter of class difference. They make us choose acquisition and fetishism over actual production or desire. They represent the *unproductive* unconscious, one that is rooted in lack of material things, such as yachts, cruises, million-dollar checks, and butlers. They are both a silencing machine and a questioning machine. They perform the American Dream of social mobility just as much as they attempt to crush political dissent. No one ever seems to question the outcome of these programs. What happens to the littlest groom after he returns from his cruise with his chosen girl? What happens to the bride's family from *My Big Fat Obnoxious Fiancé*? What happens to the actor who played the obnoxious fiancé, the would-be apprentices kicked off *The Apprentice,* and the many nonsurvivors kicked off *Survivor?* More important, what happens to the time we lost as audiences watching a hodge-podge of carefully crafted reaction shots interspersed with glamorized objects of conspicuous consumption? What are we to make of ourselves? Is class mobility possible? Is it desirable?

Class-Passing, Consumerism, and Gender

Class mobility is marked by the contradictory impulses implicit in the capitalist American Dream. On the one hand, the consumer is taught to work hard, the idea being that with pep and determination she can be upwardly mobile. On the other hand, the consumer is taught that, above all, he must be a hedonist, he must be wildly acquisitional. For capitalist society to work, we need consumers who want more and more, people who are willing to go into outrageous debt for the price of the fetishistic objects that are out of their range: McMansions, hot tubs, makeovers, couture fashion, diamonds, cruises, champagne, and luxury items. Self-discipline and hard work would seem to be at odds with hedonism, but as David Brooks argues in *Bobos in Paradise: The New Upper Class and How They Got There,* "hedonism would increasingly trump frugality, and display would increasingly replace modesty" (137). Once the shame of massive credit-card debt was removed, people started discovering that out-of-control consumption is more fun than work.

Unbridled materialism in our culture is a form of class-passing in a way. The average family has unbelievably high consumer debt, and low interest rates encourage even more debt. Also worth mentioning is that individuals are no longer referred to as "citizens," "people," or "folks." Pick up any newspaper or magazine or watch any television "journalism" and note that we are now consumers. I noticed this phenomenon in the past couple of years. It became more apparent when stories that had little to do with consumer advocacy, prices, or even consumption of products suddenly declared us all "consumers."

In a way, I suppose it is more honest. Oprah calls her audience "my people" or "my readers," when she probably should simply call them her "consumers." The product has replaced the relationship and in some cases seems to go directly toward the purchase, skipping the phase of desire or envy of the product. A print advertisement for Dove Milk Promises chocolate candies in the February 16–23, 2004, *New Yorker* asks, "What's your relationship?" and answers, below a picture of the product, "For every relationship, there's *Dove*" (209). Throughout the page, in very light typeface, we read adjectives that describe human relationships such as *playful, kinky, possessive, noncommittal,* and *steamy,* all the while knowing that our relationship is with the product. One word, *forever,* is set in boldface, designed to stand out from the rest of the ad copy. Dove promises to be there for us forever, even if other relationships turn out to be "tawdry, wacky, open or affluent."

An advertisement for the Atkins diet program in the same issue of the *New Yorker* offers a touch of class with its product, a set of four drawn-to-order *New Yorker* cartoons that actually spoof the crazed anticarbohydrate diet even as they act as little postcard ads for said same diet. On the front are the four ads on perforated cardboard. On the back is a series of pictures of the foods you can eat on the Atkins diet with the phrase "There's nothing to eat on Atkins except . . ." (95–96). I guess if the Dove Milk Promises do not deliver, one can always reach for a steak or any number of low-carb Atkins products. The funniest of the *New Yorker* cartoons has Goldilocks looking into the bowls of the three bears. The caption reads, "These are all too carb-filled." Interestingly, all four cartoons address the issue of class even beyond their status as *New Yorker* cartoons. One cartoon is set in a museum, a space of the classed, of course. Two sophisticated women decked out in fur ogle an object on display, a prehistoric woman with a sinewy body, fabulous breasts, and Pamela Anderson's hair. They are jealous of the lifeless form. One of them says in the caption, "This is prehistoric woman BC: Before Carbs." Thus the "product," a diet, becomes associated with class and the class privilege of museums. Another cartoon is set in a restaurant, probably in cosmopolitan New York. A bourgeois couple sits at a table and orders. "I'll go ahead and have the pastry chef side down." The final fourth of the page has a cartoon with men in top hats, dressed in garb associated with an earlier century. The two men are passing an old-fashioned storefront shop called "J & D Carbohydratery." The joke and the class are to be found, however, in the caption, "The King has decreed that all bakeries must change their signs. He's gone on the Atkins Diet." The ad magnificently conjures the lost aristocratic class system of the past, associating Atkins's diet with royalty, no less.

Indeed we seem to have become *Bobos in Paradise;* according to David Brooks, *bobos* are bourgeois bohemians. Because the *New Yorker* is a magazine inextricably associated with class and class privilege, we should not be surprised to find it addressing us as consumers who seek to associate ourselves with Ralph Lauren, who advertises his Polo brand on the back cover with a simple shot of a Kennedyesque suited male figure, bronzed, ready for business, a sexual icon of class-passing, probably a model class-passing for a check, probably living in a tiny hovel in New York or New Jersey, probably gay, probably more or less passing for straight, but definitely passing for elite. Like an actor, the model is another class-passer who acts as a mirror to our own class-passing. In the same issue of the *New Yorker,* the Bank of America advertises itself in a rather vulgar two-page spread featuring a close-up of a luxurious red leather portfolio against a green embossed leather desk. In today's uncertain economy, the Bank of America touts its ability to handle our supposed "wealth."

> It's no wonder we've been entrusted to manage, protect and pass on wealth for more than 150 years. . . . The Private Bank is dedicated to serving affluent families and individuals with complex wealth management needs. Our experienced advisors customize unique and comprehensive solutions for each individual, integrating world-class investment management, trusts, credit and banking service. We welcome the opportunity to work with you. We invite you to call Caroline Grace at 800.863.9500 or visit www.bankofamerica.com/privatebank. (8–9)

The Holland America Line has a four-page pull-out ad buttressing the *New Yorker*'s table of contents (14–17) and a Prada ad (12). The cruise ship line gestures to the class status we tend to think of when we invoke the art gallery. It is a close-up of a detail of a china pattern, presumably the china one would eat off if one were to book a cruise with Holland America. Before we open up the page, however, we do not know what the image is advertising. It is just the beautiful detail of a plate with the caption, "It could just as easily be hanging on an art gallery wall" (14). We turn the page and the pull-out reveals a photo of the cruise ship, the

seaworthy mobile site of everyday class-passing for the bourgeois bohe-
mian (15–17). No one knows who you are on a cruise ship. Just in case
you are worried that you might end up rubbing elbows with riffraff, the
ad mentions, "We orchestrate seamless dining experiences—enhanced by
such elegant touches as Bulgari China, linens and Riedel stemware" (16).

Shipboard class-passing is at the center of several classic films, offering the viewer a chance to experience class mobility vicariously. Itinerant
places such as ships, airports, and bus stations offer narrative opportunities for mistaken identity plot points, which often amount to class-passing. In *One Way Passage* (Tay Garnett, 1932), for example, Kay Francis,
fatally ill, falls for con man and class-passer William Powell. Francis's
numerous on-screen characters constantly fell in love with people who
were not at all what they appeared to be. On screen, at least, she would
do well to stay away from luxury liners, casino halls, and in fact just about
any public space where she might fall for a class-passer.

Perhaps one of the more interesting class-passing vehicles is a film starring Kay Francis. The stylish and opulent decor and design of *Trouble in
Paradise* (Ernst Lubitsch, 1932) serves as the backdrop for the story of
Gaston Monescu (Herbert Marshall), a common jewel thief who class-
passes as a sort of foreign-born royal. His lover, brilliantly played by
Miriam Hopkins (as Lily Vautier), is also his partner in crime. Together
they try to bilk chic industrialist Mariette Colet (Kay Francis) out of a
small fortune. Class-passing moves in all directions in this delightful comedy. At times, Hopkins class-passes downward as Kay Francis's maid, all
the better to get closer to poor Mariette Colet's jewels and help Monescu
steal from the rich widow's safe. Herbert Marshall also gets to class-pass
downward when he takes a job as the widow's secretary. Nothing is as it
seems, and no one is who he or she says they are in *Trouble in Paradise*.
The film opens with a sort of aural joke on class-passing. We hear offscreen
what we assume to be an operatic gondolier but soon learn that he is
merely a garbage collector. Perhaps Lubitsch, having come from Europe,
was a good outside observer of the limits of the American class system.
His humor is steeped in leftist ideology, yet it is displayed with the light
touch of the most brilliant of safecrackers. Poor Mariette Colet falls head
over heels for her burglar, thereby allowing Hopkins and Marshall to
escape the law. The passion shown by Hopkins and Marshall is given a
great deal of frisson from their competitive class-passing. They try to outdo
each other in crime and respect one another's ability to pull off class-passing and theft undetectably.

One never knows where one is going to run into the class-passer. The delightfully elegant William Powell is passing as a tramp when Carole Lombard picks him up in Gregory LaCava's *My Man Godfrey* (1936). The script, by Morrie Ryskind and Eric Match, opens with a cruel twist on the popular Depression-era America pastime of the "treasure hunt." Two Park Avenue brats, Carole Lombard and Gail Patrick (as Irene and Cornelia Bullock), compete to bring home a forgotten man. Mistaking the class-passing Godfrey "Duke" Parke (William Powell) for a hobo, the two women fight over him. Lombard wins, and she brings him home to be the family butler. In a delightfully crazy bit of multiple class-passing, we enjoy watching Powell, who as a real-life actor we know is rather classed, play a wealthy man who pretends to be a bum playing a butler but who is really a bored industrialist.

My Man Godfrey takes potshots at the rich: the portrayals of the worthless, idle mother; the grumbling, unhappy father who manages to lose the family fortune and has to be saved by the so-called butler; and the two young women who spend their lives drinking, partying, and dressing. Mischa Auer, as Carlo, is fantastic as an utterly useless hanger-on who insists he is a painter despite his never having produced a single work of art. LaCava carefully includes the waitstaff's reactions, which are much like the reaction shots of the family in *The Simple Life*. Alan Mowbray and Jean Dixon steal the scene at times with their eye rolling. Temporary class-passing often helps a richer character grow up, as it does in the case of Godfrey. Because of his contact with the poor and disenfranchised, as well as his contact with the idle rich, he becomes politically aware and motivated to change things and he does.

The hypocrisy of the rich is a common theme in the Depression-era films of the 1930s. One memorable effort is Wanda Tuchock's *Finishing School* (1934), which features a very young Ginger Rogers and Frances Dee, both of whom attend an exclusive upper-crust girl's school where hypocrisy is an everyday routine. Bruce Cabot is a struggling young hospital intern from a questionable background who falls in love with Frances Dee. *Finishing School* is almost an American version of Leontine Sagan's German film classic, *Mådchen in Uniform* (1931). In *Finishing School*, Billie Burke plays a horrid upper-class mother who shows no love for her daughter, Frances Dee. (Society mothers are usually depicted as uncaring in American film and popular culture.) The title itself becomes ironic and points to the tragedy of the plight of the unloved society girl, who herself is socially "finished" by the end of the narrative. Ginger Rogers plays a bad society girl who teaches Dee (as Virginia) to smoke, lie, cheat, drink, and date smarmy rich boys. But Dee becomes pregnant after a one-night affair with Bruce Cabot, a waiter working his way through medical school. Predictably, everyone disapproves of a match between the wealthy young Dee and Cabot. Dee's destructive mother will not allow the wedding, so Dee attempts suicide. Cabot and Dee's father, who comes to accept the good working-class doctor-in-training, rescue her. The burden of policing class often falls on the mother and women in general. The father in *My Man Godfrey* easily accepts his daughter's love for someone out of her class. Women are often the guardians of class and class-passing and thus are often subject to harsher enforcement of the rules of society. This paradox is true in so many films, from Michael Curtiz's *Mildred Pierce* (1945) to Ida Lupino's *Hard, Fast and Beautiful* (1951), and is also true of the reality show *My Big Fat Obnoxious Fiancé*.

Female class-passers often work to envision a home, usually a better-class home, a wealthier home, a status of being at home with their new classed body. The class-passing body is sometimes subject to the same sort of rejection as that of those passing across race: "The passer whose success emerged from his utter rejection of community thus felt the full brunt of that same rejection, and it decimated all of his accomplishments" (Pfeiffer 148). Women's films of the 1930s and 1940s show many examples of the rejected class-passer whose minstrelsy is displayed and rejected.

Indeed, the foregrounding of class difference (poverty versus opulence) is exhibited and performed by women who cross barriers or make melodramatic sacrifices so that their children might effectively "class-pass" in many films of the 1930s and early 1940s, such as Frank Capra's *Forbidden* (1932), Edgar Selwyn's *The Sin of Madelon Claudet* (1931), Lloyd Bacon and Michael Curtiz's *Marked Woman* (1937), and King Vidor's *Stella Dallas* (1937). Performing gender and performing modernism in these films are inextricably linked to the narrative, the characters, and the world they inhabit. One might argue that modernism itself is defined as elite, classed, and sleekly designed (evidenced by the sets and costumes), as well as gendered, in these films. Women in the films have designs on wealth and harbor the modernist American Dream of moving up in class status. Modernist principles of mechanization are implied in the performed examples of myriad ritualized acts of self-stylization against a backdrop of sleek, classically designed period costumes and accessories, as much as they are juxtaposed against the opposing constructs of realism, sexism, and classism.

Class rise itself was problematic to the censors of the day. As Lea Jacobs writes, "the MPPDA [Motion Picture Producers and Distributors of America] repeatedly warned producers that the heroine's rise in class, particularly in [John M. Stahl's] *Back Street* (1932), would make a film vulnerable to public criticism" (108). The MPPDA Code, enforced in the mid-1930s, seemed to be more than obsessed with the power of motion pictures to appeal to and perhaps disrupt the masses or multitudes of every class. The Code sidestepped such specific labels as *lower class, middle class,* and *upper class* (which, more accurately, should have read *lower income, middle income,* and *upper income*). Instead, the framers divide the class structure into three binarisms: "mature/immature, developed/undeveloped and law-abiding/criminal" (Doherty 349). In the MPPDA Code appendix, the writers address the "special moral obligations" in the area of class with regard to the motion picture. This section repeatedly emphasizes the mobility of film and its ability to reach "every class," "places unpenetrated by other forms of art," and the difficulty of producing films "intended for only certain classes of people":

The motion picture has special Moral obligations:

(A) Most arts appeal to the mature. This art appeals at once to every class—mature, immature, developed, undeveloped, law-abiding, criminal. Music has its grades for different classes; so has literature and drama. This art of the motion picture, combining as it does the two fundamental appeals of looking at a picture and listening to a story, at once reaches every class of society.

(B) Because of the mobility of a film and the ease of picture distribution, and because of the possibility of duplicating positives in large quantities, this art reaches places unpenetrated by other forms of art.

(C) Because of these two facts, it is difficult to produce films intended for only *certain classes of people.* The exhibitor's theatres are built for the masses, for the cultivated and the rude, mature and immature, self-restrained and inflammatory, young and old, law-respecting and criminal. Films, unlike books and music, can with difficulty be confined to certain selected groups.

(D) The latitude given to film material cannot, in consequence, be as wide as the latitude given to *book material.* (Doherty 349; emphasis in original)

Thus the code alludes to the power of modern cinema to break with traditions designed to conserve the constituency of the leisure classes by admitting even the immature, undeveloped, and criminal element into the world of the leisure class. As Thorstein Veblen argued, class-passing was meant to be only by selective admission.

> The constituency of the leisure class is kept up by a continual selective process, whereby the individuals and lines of descent that are eminently fitted for an aggressive pecuniary competition are withdrawn from the lower classes. In order to reach the upper levels the aspirant must have, not only a fair average complement of the pecuniary aptitudes, but he [also] must have these gifts in such an eminent degree as to overcome very material difficulties that stand in the way of his ascent. Barring accidents, the *nouveaux arrivés* are a picked body. (144)

But, as Veblen also noted, "tenacity and consistency of aim" (145) were also distinguished qualities of the "successful predatory barbarian" (145) or class-passer.

This was never truer than in the modernist era. Perhaps no one in the cinema has quite as much tenacity, single-mindedness, and consistency of aim as the main character of Alfred E. Green's *Baby Face* (1933), Lily, brilliantly portrayed by Barbara Stanwyck. *Baby Face* concerns a gold-digging young woman from a small town who uses her brains and sexuality to move up the economic ladder. As the film's tagline notes, "she climbed the ladder of success—wrong by wrong." Thomas Doherty dubs the film "the most notorious of the sex-in-the-workplace vice films of the pre-Code era" (134). Jeanine Basinger sees *Baby Face* as "a classic example of a movie in which a woman climbs over men to the top" (266).

Whereas most readings of the film understandably emphasize Lily's use of sexuality to conquer and rise to the top, perhaps it is also her blatant embrace of *modernism* and its brazen capitalist predatory zeal and Art Deco style that ensure her success. In addition, Stanwyck takes to the role with a gusto that is contagious; her portrayal shows a Lily who is not the slightest bit ashamed of the human mechanics behind her rise to power. The audience easily identifies with her struggle to get ahead in the midst of the Great Depression, particularly when she beds and then discards a young John Wayne (in the role of midlevel executive Jimmy McCoy Jr.) on her way to the top of the corporate ladder.

Lily embraces the hardening process of the big city, which is alluded to in the MPPDA censorship code: "Small communities, remote from sophistication and from the hardening process which often takes place in the ethical and moral standards of larger cities, are easily and readily reached by any sort of film" (350).

Lily not only seduces men on her way to the top but also conquers the modern city skyscraper, floor by floor, as the camera cuts to an exterior of the Art Deco "Gotham Trust Company" each time she successfully manages to obtain a better job through seduction, flirtation, and a change in her appearance, all to embrace American modernism. The modern skyscraper embodies Lily; it is in turn emblematic of her hardening process, her quick-change class-passing from a tramp with old-fashioned clothing and hair to a dazzling bleached blonde, Deco-gowned modern woman. In forging her identity, Lily embodies the problematic emergence of modernist emphasis on capitalism, luxury, and Art Deco. As Mike O'Mahoney writes, "Despite this utopian emphasis on luxury, Art Deco emerged in an era of economic slumps and depressions, social strife, hunger marches and the political battle between Communism and Fascism. It was against this troubled and traumatic backdrop that Art Deco forged its own identity" (6).

Lily's traumatic and troubled backstory includes being forced to turn tricks by her father, who runs a speakeasy. Not surprising, Lily has no interest in the past. She moves forward with the passion and tenacity of a luxury liner. She makes fun of the snobbery of the old-fashioned Emily Post. She's interested only in the future, her future. Her friend Adolf Cragg (Alphonse Ethier), a sort of German mentor, encourages her to read Nietzsche. "You must be a master, not a slave," he tells her. But her embrace of the future betrays her class origins, for as Paul Fussell reminds us, "Classy people never deal with the future. That's for vulgarians like traffic engineers, planners and inventors" (72). Instead, only monied characters are interested in what Veblen termed "veneration of the archaic," as Fussell explains (72).

Lily has *no* interest in studying Nietzsche as if he were a classical antiquity; instead, she parlays his ideas into modernist capitalist ideology. Her class-passing is dependent on trampling anyone in her way. Indeed, perhaps her single-minded aspiration for wealth and luxury was most highly problematic to the censors. In Lea Jacobs's study of the censorship of *Baby Face*, Jacobs notes that "the MPPDA repeatedly warned producers that the heroine's rise in class would make a film vulnerable to public criticism" (108). Hollywood's chief censor, Joseph Breen, in particular "seems to have agreed with his predecessors that class rise presented a problem for the [film] industry" (Jacobs 108). Jacobs dismisses her own evidence and concludes that "from the perspective of the MPPDA, showing a character become rich was not, in and of itself, a point of difficulty" (109).

Instead, Jacobs highlights the inherent attractiveness of the immoral gold digger "insofar as her movement in class united a certain image of money and power with illicit sexuality" (109). Nonetheless, given the language and ideology of the code, emphasizing the censors' class jitters with regard to a script and a film preoccupied with class rise might be interesting.

Class opposition, breaking the borders of class, whether in gangster films or in gold-digging films, brings about the specter of possibilities for class mobility and, at the very least, a critique of the class-gender system. Chuck Kleinhans writes,

> When we look at the emergence of the modern melodrama about 250 years ago (the bourgeois domestic melodrama, to be more precise), today everyone can clearly understand its class nature as drama of and for a specific class, posed against another class: a cultural-ideological weapon in a political and economic struggle that change history forever. (198)

Not all critics agree. But even Charles Eckert, who sees class position as only temporal or fleeting in films such as *Marked Woman*, points out the sharp delineation of the spectacle of class opposition.

> If class opposition is regarded as seminal, its displacement into ethical, regional and other oppositions can be seen as both the result of conscious censorship and a myth-like transposition of the conflict into new terms. The latter is an unconscious or less conscious procedure whereby the *force* of the opposition is diminished while its form and some of its substance are retained. The effect in the film is for the ethical and regional dilemmas to function as displaced, and partly defused, class oppositions. They can still *feel* like class oppositions and be treated as such by the writers and director; the city with its penthouses and limousines can function as reified capitalism; wittiness can be allied to the manipulations of financiers; all of this can be given high resolution by the use of visual coding—skyscrapers, tuxedos, one-hundred-dollar bills; but every thrust of class or economic protest is sufficiently blunted to avoid breaking the skin. (217)

However, from a feminist perspective, *Marked Woman* is a perfect example of outright puncturing of the skin of class. This feminist classic revolves around the struggles of a group of prostitutes led by the central figure Mary Dwight (Bette Davis), who works in a sleazy clip joint to send her sister, Betty (Jane Bryan), to boarding school. Betty, who is completely unaware of her sister's occupation and her own complicity in the situation, arrives unannounced for a visit. At Mary's insistence, the women pretend to be fashion models. But Betty ends up class-passing downward when she goes to a party and is drawn to the allure of the nightlife of gangsters. She wears one of the girl's swanky Deco dresses and is impressed by the Deco nightclub and penthouse of Johnny Vanning (Eduardo Cianelli), a vicious mob lord based on Charles "Lucky" Luciano, the Depression-era mafioso who ruled by terrorism. Meanwhile, as Betty gets sucked into the glamour of the nightlife, her sister, Mary, agrees to testify against Johnny Vanning. Betty finally figures out that her sister is really a clip joint B-girl and part-time prostitute. She is suspended between class strata when the newspapers carry the story and she believes she cannot return to school. In her anger and despair, Betty lashes out at her sister and goes off to a party at Vanning's, where Vanning kills her as she struggles to evade his sexual advances. Her downward class-passing in fact brings about her murder. Vanning accuses her of putting on airs when she does not submit to his sexual come-ons. He punches her for "putting on an act," and she falls down a short flight of stairs to her death. When Mary learns of her sister's death, she vows to get Vanning. She confronts him, his thugs beat her, and she is marked with a horrible gash on her face in the form of an X, a sign that she is an enemy of Vanning.

Without her beauty, viciously beaten, and recovering in the hospital, Mary finally decides to cooperate with the district attorney, Graham, played by Humphrey Bogart. She vows to testify against Vanning and persuades her roommates to testify as well. After Vanning is convicted, Graham, who has demonstrated an interest in Mary, approaches her on the courtroom stairs. One might expect an impossibly happy ending: Graham and Mary sharing a romantic kiss and a wedding proposal. But this pre-Code film gives us a realistic ending, one that clearly raises the specter of class difference. In their conversation, Mary abruptly dismisses Graham's proposal because of their class difference. After Mary congratulates him, he responds.

> *Graham:* You're the one who should be getting the congratulations, not me.
> *Mary:* Um-um. I don't want them.
> *Graham:* But where will you go?
> *Mary:* Places.
> *Graham:* But what will you do?
> *Mary:* Oh, I'll get along, I always have.

Graham: Mary, I'd like to help you.

Mary: (curious . . . and interested) Why?

Graham: Why . . . because I . . . because I think you've got a break
comin' to you.

Mary: (still curious) And?

Graham: And I'd like to see that you get it.

Mary: (suddenly dejected) What's the use of stalling? We both live in
different worlds, and that's the way we've got to leave it.

Graham: I don't want to leave it that way. I once said to you that if you
ever started helping yourself I'd be the first one to go to bat for you,
and that still goes. No matter what you do or where you go, we'll
meet again.

Mary: Goodbye, Graham. I'll be seeing you. (quoted in Eckert 211–12)

Mary's recognition that they both live in different worlds is an acknowl-
edgment that class-passing is nearly impossible for the fallen woman. After
the conversation, Mary joins the other women who have testified. Blues
music swells on the soundtrack as they are surrounded by mist from studio fog machines. The bravery and sisterhood with which they face the
world is truly compelling. Eckert calls *Marked Woman* "vintage *cinéma
brut*" but, as mentioned, regards the film's class opposition as limited. I'd
assert that the film's ending is powerful agit-prop. Just because the women
accept their fate, the audience may not. In fact this grim ending, which
starkly points out the realities of gender and class in the Depression era,
incites in the audience a call for change from the status quo much more
than a falsely romantic heterotopic union might.

Marked Woman takes aim not only at the exploitative capitalist patri-
archal system but also at modernism. If modernism comes at the expense
of human life, what is the point of fast cars, enormous Deco penthouses,
luxurious gowns, champagne, and progress? We find no easy answers to
the questions posed in *Marked Woman*. Instead, the film insists that the
burden of class struggle sits at the feet of the audience, who must speak
out just as the women who testified against Vanning spoke out. *Marked
Woman*, like *Baby Face*, is a damning film. It damns the audience and calls
for change—the type of change T. W. Adorno calls for in his classic tract
about the culture industry.

Only their deep unconscious is trust, the last residue of the difference
between art and empirical reality in the spiritual make-up of the masses
explains why they have not, to a person, long since perceived and accepted

the world as it is constructed for them by the culture industry. . . . If the masses have been unjustly reviled from above as masses, the culture industry is not among the least responsible for making them into masses and then despising them, while obstructing the emancipation for which human beings are as ripe as the productive forces of the epoch permit. (60)

Films such as *Baby Face* and *Marked Woman* do not abide by the code of the culture industry. They emphasize the trauma implicit in the modernist paradigm, a trauma steeped in economic strife, classism, sexism, ageism, and the perils of class-passing, set against the binaries of squalor versus luxury and glamour. Fallen-women films of the pre-Code era exposed the dangers of glamour and luxury. Lea Jacobs concludes,

> What is clear however is that the fallen woman cycle was defined and discussed similarly outside of the industry—in popular and academic sources—and within the industry, by the MPPDA censors. All of these sources employ terms such as "glamour" and "luxury" and there is general agreement that the cycle undermines accepted moral/sexual norms through the heroine's rise to wealth. (109)

This is not to suggest, however, that certain ambivalence does not run through these films in their sociopolitical messages. *Baby Face,* for example, suffers from a tacked-on ending in which Lily suddenly does an about-face to save her man. It is such an unbelievable Hollywood ending that some female spectators simply refuse to accept it, remember it, or acknowledge it. Betsy Israel, writing in *Bachelor Girl: The Secret History of Single Women in the Twentieth Century,* omits it in her summary of the film.

> In *Baby Face* . . . a heartless-woman masterpiece, Barbara Stanwyck, a speakeasy bartender, puts on a decent dress and works her way up within a corporation, starting on the first floor as a filing clerk. We know immediately that she's an operator. She casually asks a colleague how she got *such* a great perm. She asks another one where she got the *fabulous* shoes. She shows up with the perm and identical shoes the next day. Soon she's headed up the corporate skyscraper. On each new floor (accounting, mortgages, et cetera) she's transformed: better clothes and hairstyles, an entirely new professional manner. At each stop she lures then abruptly drops at least one ardent lover, although one man she keeps around—a strategist and booster, who's advised her and helped

finance her climb. Finally we see her at the top, draped in one of those sparkly floor-length gowns so many thirties heroines wore just to swish around the house. In this key scene, the lover and friend charges into her office. He needs cash. He's desperate. And he asks her point blank for some jewels he once helped her buy. She stares at him. Thinks. And then she delivers a heartless-woman manifesto: "I have to think of myself. I've gone through a lot to get those things. My life has been bitter and hard. I'm not like other women. All the gentleness and kindness in me has been killed. All I've got is those things. Without them, I'd be nothing. . . . I'd have to go back to what I was! No! I won't do it, I tell you, I won't." And she doesn't. (157)

But the truth is that she does. As Jeanine Basinger accurately points out, "throughout this film, there has been no indication that Stanwyck is the woman she becomes in the final five minutes" (270). Basinger is perplexed, as audiences must have been, by the abrupt departure in the narrative of *Baby Face*.

What we have seen and the way we are asked to view it are not completely matched. In the end, of course, Stanwyck becomes a "real woman." She has wept, given back the jewelry, and accepted her position of slave, not master. Love will not be her career. The ultimate irony of this astonishing movie is the very ending. Brent and Stanwyck are back in Erie, Pennsylvania, in the same factory slums she began in. The final image of the movie is the identical skyline of the coalfields that was visible in the first moments of the film. Stanwyck has progressed exactly nowhere. (270)

Perhaps Israel can be forgiven her lapse of accuracy, given the tacked-on nature of the end. More important, however, is that Israel's more feminist ending easily could have been the favored method of spectatorship of the film when it was released. Audiences coproduce meaning of a text, and women audiences are perfectly capable of constructing (or reconstituting) their own endings. When I show this film to my students, for example, at the University of Nebraska, they, too, have a way of dispensing with the ending, easily linking it to censorship. In paper after paper, students say they prefer to simply disregard the false "happy" ending, just as they embrace the ending of *Marked Woman* as a strong feminist critique of gender and class and disagree with Charles Eckert's estimation of the film as a failed or, at least, muddled Marxist tract.

With regard to moral complexity, feminist ambiguity, and messages of class-passing, the maternal melodrama frustrates most contemporary students. Admittedly, it is problematic as a feminist genre, in that it manages both to value and to devalue women, particularly mothers. Linda Williams asserts, "The device of devaluing and debasing the actual figure of the mother while sanctifying the institution of motherhood is typical of the 'woman's film' in general and the subgenre of the maternal melodrama in particular" (308). Christian Viviani suggests that the maternal melodrama can be experienced on different levels.

> In sum, the maternal melo plays—sometimes with a certain cunning—on two levels. It seems outwardly attached to the old moral code by making the mother pay for her 'sin.' But it implicitly condemns the old system of values represented by a sterile or unhappy couple, which is obliged to adopt the bastard child in order to offer up the image of a traditional family. (94)

Basinger, however, sees the possibility for a more radical and certainly more subversive reading of the maternal melodrama.

> A movie plot in which a woman has to give up her child provided a two-way street of response for viewers who were mothers, perhaps feeling burdened with the difficulties of raising their own children. A woman on film who sacrifices a child suffers and is ultimately punished, reassuring the women watching. At the same time, the woman on film who gives up a child suddenly has freedom. Often, she finds a better life of riches, success, adventure, and, in the end, even an opportunity for love with another man or the same man who caused her problem in the first place. The viewer could watch a woman get free of the burden of mothering without having to feel guilty about it. (395)

The maternal melodrama is amazingly formulaic considering its effectiveness. The list of remarkable maternal melodramas includes *Forbidden* (1932), in which Barbara Stanwyck falls for an unhappily married attorney (Adolph Menjou). She gives birth to his child and allows his wife to adopt the child, thus ensuring that her offspring will effectively class-pass into a world of wealth and security. Similarly, in *The Sin of Madelon Claudet* (1931), Helen Hayes is an unwed mother forced into prostitution to raise her son. Kay Francis covers for her daughter, who accidentally kills a man in Robert Florey's *The House on 56th Street* (1933). She similarly gives up her life for her child in *I Found Stella Parrish* (Mervyn

LeRoy, 1935). Gladys George and Ruth Chatterton give up their lives for their offspring in two of the many versions of *Madame X* (directed by Lionel Barrymore in 1929 and by Sam Wood and Gustav Machaty in 1937). Chatterton allows herself to be executed to ensure her son's social status as district attorney (who convicts her and allows her to be executed) in William Wellman's *Frisco Jenny* (1932). And Barbara Stanwyck gives up all rights to her child in *Stella Dallas* so that she, too, can experience the privileges of status and social class.

All these mothers wage war on the class system. They are strong role models of martyrdom and valiant heroes with which women could identify. Because these mothers show their suffering, many feminist critics and contemporary audiences cannot stomach their martyrdom. But in their suffering they supersede gender roles as a class. If we compare their suffering with that of male heroes in war movies, for example, they emerge as figures to be admired if not emulated. If we can but suspend our own moral outrage at their endless and complete suffering, we can find examples of some of the strongest women on celluloid. We must not doubly punish them because of their gender.

Male heroes in comparable roles are celebrated and held up as exemplifications of archetypal heroes. Fallen women's actions condemn the old system of values on which gender and class oppression depend. This issue is not so much that I enjoy watching them in their child-free states, often shown aboard luxury liners, enjoying bachelor adventures, or skirting the boundaries of expected female norms of behavior (which I do); it is instead that I also value their iconicity as strong role models who outwit the system in the best ways they can. It is especially the social class system that they attack and subvert, and if we read them within a different context, within their own terms, *they win.*

Stella Dallas (Barbara Stanwyck) is triumphant when she walks away from her daughter as the latter weds into a socially connected family. Min (Marie Dressler) is similarly triumphant in George W. Hill's *Min and Bill* (1930) when she walks away, bound for prison, knowing that she has beaten the system. Her adopted daughter will never know that her real mother was a drunken prostitute and that Min has murdered her to protect her daughter from her. Ruth Chatterton's son (Donald Cook) will never know that his mother in *Frisco Jenny* chose not to fight a murder charge against her so that she may protect his innocence, thereby ensuring his social status as a district attorney bound for the mayor's office. Barbara Stanwyck is a tower of strength as she walks away from her child in *Forbidden* and later in *Stella Dallas*. When Vergie Winters (Ann Harding) falls in love with married politician John Shadwell (John Boles) in Alfred Santell's *The Life of Vergie Winters* (1934), she refuses to hinder his career, even when she becomes pregnant. Vergie is content with a backstreet romance, while their class-passing daughter, Joan, grows up in ignorance of her birth mother's true identity. The class-passing children of Madelon Claudet, Stella Parish, Vergie Winters, Madame X, and all the Madame X's will neither have to face the grinding mill of poverty, sexual abuse, neglect, or the race, gender, and class oppression their mothers suffered nor ever really know how their mothers beat the oppressive American class system and triumphed as heroines, but the audiences will and do know.

On a more symbolic level, the audience, aware of the triumph of these celluloid mothers, also becomes distinctly aware of the realities of the class system and its supporting structures, such as racism, gender discrimination, and the marriage system. Depression-era escapist fare, on the other hand, offered the proletariat a panacea from thinking about disturbing political issues. As bell hooks notes, consumer culture does the cultural work of silencing discussion about class. But class does matter, she insists.

> Consumer culture silences working people and the middle classes. They are busy buying or planning to buy. Although their fragile hold on economic self-sufficiency is slipping, they still cling to the dream of a class-free society where everyone can make it to the top. They are afraid to face the significance of dwindling resources, the high cost of education, housing, and health care. They are afraid to think too deeply about class. At the end of the day, the threat of class warfare, of class struggle, is just too dangerous to face. (6)

The children who successfully class-pass in melodramas of the 1930s prove Rita Felski's observation that "a person from a lower-class background who has acquired education and money might be said to pass as middle or upper class in the same way as a gay man or lesbian can pass as straight" (38). Again, class-passing shares things in common with gender- and race-passing and is also related to drag and cross-dressing. Indeed, successful class-passing, even when dependent on the sacrificial mother figure, *proves* that class is a *fabrication*.

To borrow from Judith Butler's work on the performative nature of gender, I think revisiting her most important and revolutionary work—the chapter "Subversive Bodily Acts" in *Gender Trouble*—is helpful here. In the following passages, I have substituted the word *class* for the word *gender* to display how Butler's methodology, when applied to class, disrupts the notion of coherency and stability when it comes to class, just as it disrupts the gender binary system.

> If the inner truth of [class] is a fabrication and if true [class] is a fantasy instituted and inscribed on the surface of bodies, then it seems that [classes] can be neither true nor false, but are only produced as the truth effects of a discourse of primary and stable identity. . . . In imitating [class], drag implicitly reveals the imitative striker of [class] itself—as well as its contingency. (174–75)

Thus, whereas Butler overhauls the idea of original or true gender identity, I have used her words to disrupt the notion of immutable class identity. Class, like gender, may be construed as a socially constructed and regulated series of performed acts and gestures. One might say, then, that actual wealth is necessary to perform class, but that is not always necessarily true, just as enacting gender through biological evidence is not always necessary. Using Butler, we can conclude that class norms are in many ways a fiction disguised as a truth and that the perimeters of class are patrolled just as regularly as those of gender.

The maternal melodramas of the Depression era allowed viewers a peek into, or even a road map of, the nature of class mobility. The finales of these films highlight the effectiveness of class drag and class-passing, usually through the marriage system or the education system. In *Min and Bill*, the title characters step aside as their adopted wharf rat of a girl, Nancy (Dorothy Jordan), learns how to class-pass. She stops chewing gum and shouting. She learns to speak differently, she learns to dress better, and she goes away to boarding school to learn manners and other proper behavior. She meets a young man of the aristocracy, who marries her. But class-passing, like gender- and race-passing, can be painful and family-shattering. When Nancy comes home to visit Min and Bill, Min breaks all ties with the girl, bringing into sharp relief the pain and hardship that both the class-passer and the facilitating mother figure must endure. The pain is registered indelibly on the face of Marie Dressler, who won an Academy Award for her performance. Min, who has a chance to escape a murder charge, remains on the wharf just long enough to see her adopted daughter marry up.

Marrying up, however, is not just painted as a positive step of class-passing. The upward mobility of the child comes with a price, and both the parent and child pay that price—the pain of permanent separation.

Nancy, as with many of the child class-passers, is not well delineated as a full character. As my students have pointed out to me, the children in maternal melodramas are often not fully fleshed out. They are more like concepts of personalities, and in that way they are also glimpses of class drag. Their incomplete personalities are like modernist paintings of light and shadow, dapples of color that barely connect as full human beings, especially when contrasted with the more fully characterized mother figures. Perhaps these class-passing children best exemplify the fragmented and incomplete identities of the self as redefined in modernist literature.

Similarly, Barbara Stanwyck's daughter in *Stella Dallas*, Laurel (Anne Shirley), becomes less interesting, less complex, and less a full character as she attains class status. The social climber is increasingly boring and bored by her mother's behavior. When she goes to live with her rich father and his upper-class wife and Stella comes to visit, Laurel is permitted some bit of character, that of a selfish little snob, who is increasingly embarrassed by her real mother's gaudy wardrobe. Indeed, *Stella Dallas* is interesting in the maternal melo cycle in that Stella does not simply make a quick disappearance. Instead, she hangs around the picture, acting inappropriately, being made fun of by the rich kids at the club, and embarrassing her daughter.

In a devastating scene of class rupture, mother and daughter are returning home on a train. In her compartment, Stella overhears the rich young aesthetes making fun of her, "Laurel's horrible mother." Laurel, burdened by class fissure, climbs into her mother's compartment to console her and display her loyalty. Later Stella pretends to be a hopeless drunk in an instance of downward class minstrelsy to push her daughter away. She "performs" lower class drag in even more outlandish and cheap clothing and pretends to smoke, gamble, and sleep with a shabby bum (played by Alan Hale).

Stella Dallas is morally superior to anyone in the film. John Boles, who plays Laurel's father, is cold, awkward, and unfeeling. His wife, however, is more fleshed out and sympathetic. Barbara O'Neil, who plays Boles's wife, Helen Morrison, is at first portrayed as barren, rich, and idle. But she learns morality from Stella and ensures that Stella can watch her daughter marry by carefully opening the mansion's draperies. That the wedding is framed by a picture window highlights Laurel's effective class-passing for the audience. The image of Barbara Stanwyck in shabby clothes, a tear in her eye, as a cop asks her to move on, is indelibly stamped in the audience's memories. But she is a triumphant woman, a complete hero. Her sacrifice is as great as or greater than that of any male hero of the day. Even my most resistant male student, tired of the maternal melo formula, fell for this film.

Laurel is left to wonder why her mother has not shown up for the wedding. Laurel, along with Min and Bill's adopted daughter, Nancy, feels the pain and legacy of class-passing through the marriage system. Other children who successfully class-pass as a result of the efforts of maternal melodramas do so via education, be it for the legal profession or the medical profession. Male figures in these films, however, are often clueless about class politics, and again something about them seems underdeveloped and false. The wooden performance of Donald Cook, who plays the title character's son Dan in *Frisco Jenny* is a good example. Pregnant and alone, Jenny has lost her fiancé and her father during the San Francisco earthquake. She tries to survive by working as a prostitute and allows her son to be adopted by a "good family." Soon Jenny is one of the leading madams in the rackets. When she sees that her son, who does not even know her, has a chance to become a successful district attorney, she turns in the crooks around her. When one of the crooks threatens to expose her identity as Dan's mother, she shoots him. She offers no explanation on the witness stand. As a viewer, you are torn between the desire for her to speak up and save herself and the understanding that she is a heroine protecting her son. But in William Wellman's cold retelling of the *Madame X* formula, she never reveals her identity and goes to the electric chair so that her son may successfully class-pass. Once again, effective class-passing is dependent on the erasure of the strong-willed sacrificing mother, here brilliantly played by Ruth Chatterton.

Helen Hayes plays an almost identical role in *The Sin of Madelon Claudet,* who sacrifices all for her illegitimate son, played by the stiff cardboard cutout Robert Young. Hayes won an Academy Award for her portrayal of a suffering mother reduced to a haggard streetwalker. Gladys George turns in another remarkably strong performance in *Madame X* (1937). Her husband, played by Warren William, has thrown her out of the house and is unable to forgive her one infidelity. She ends up on the streets and becomes mixed up in a murder. She is threatened by the snarling Lerocle (Henry Daniell), who tries to blackmail her into owning up to her identity as the mother of Raymond Fleuriot (John Beal), a promising young lawyer. Fleuriot, stiff and hollow, ends up trying to defend her on a murder charge, but she never reveals her true identity to her son. She is saved from the gallows only by a fatal heart attack in the judge's chambers, just before sentence is passed.

Perhaps it is important that the class-passing child is not fully characterized, because any commitment to the lower class and any excess emotion betray one's humble class background. Maternal melodramas give us a blank character, perfect for class drag because she or he has seemingly so little to hide. The burden of hiding class-passing is placed firmly on the shoulders of the mother. She can and has been read as the victim, but one also may view her as the ultimate hero of American individualism. She embraces change, she embraces the future, and she enables class-passing for her spawn. Class-passing, finally, is seen as a dangerous but possible act in Depression-era films. Class-passing is celebrated and displayed, only to be ritually punished in the end. In a gendered context, the class-passing subject is seen as a threat to the social order, even as his or her success within the film's narrative is celebrated. Issues of fragmentation and one's identity are not always easily glossed over. The class-passing identity can come apart easily if just one thread is pulled from her newly constructed self. In the modernist realm, the best way to class-pass effectively is to marry or reproduce. Ironically, the greatest sacrifice is to marry up, reproduce, and disappear, leaving a motherless child who can fully class-pass.

3
Class-Passing and
Negotiations of
Masculinity

The vision of a little boy in a tuxedo or a business suit is not just incongruous but singularly ridiculous. The young boy performs a minstrelsy of classed manhood that never quite works. Although women are often constructed in popular culture as the guardians of class and the family, men and manhood are ineluctably connected to class performativity. Put simply, men are born to class-pass in capitalist culture. For men, adulthood is inherently associated with a Darwinian business model of class rise. Think of the markers of masculine rites of passage into manhood and note how they are linked to class.

Traditional societal roles define men as breadwinners, wage earners who are responsible for the family and its social mobility. Before he even gets to this point, the man moves through several class-passing negotiations of masculinity. Take dating, for example. Isn't dating a form of class drag? Although the rituals have become less codified in terms of gender, the heterosexual traditional "date" of the past depended on a man's ability to spend money on a young woman, often money he had earned for the first time. Before the young girl will agree to a date, however, in so many popular culture narratives, the young man must prove he has money and can purchase a fancy car. The automobile becomes not just a consumerist fantasy but a vehicle for class-passing. Consequently, many stories depend on this series of events: the young man must get his first job to get his first car to get his first date. It is a class-passing drama that has been enacted by every actor from Laurel and Hardy to Jim Carrey.

Looking across the vast spectrum of images of men in popular culture, I am struck by the number of images of maleness as drag and of masculinity that is so intertwined with means that I have to conclude that male value is often constructed on the basis of this ability to consume, class-pass, and present the objects that they have been able to acquire, whether they are expensive "toys," such as computers, cell phones, and portable DVD players, or automobiles and business suits.

Popular culture uses humor to express that about which we feel discomfort. The Three Stooges' entire career was dependent on making a mockery of the expectations put on maleness in terms of employment and class mobility. Many critics have noticed that almost every two-reel short comedy the Three Stooges made has them getting and losing a job (in and of itself a class-pass) or a series of jobs to "get the girl." The Three Stooges spend considerable screen time playing like little boys. Their antics go against the grain of the expectations put on young men who are taught to behave, be strong, respect authority, speak correct English, and wear adult clothing. Curly's oft-imitated cries of "whoo, whoo, whoo," Moe's consistent "unpleasability," and Larry's air of blank detachment are uniquely infantile.

Instead of using violence to acquire goods, the Three Stooges slap each other constantly, in a way slapping each other down economically. One cannot very well class-pass, much less "get the girl," after all, if one has a black eye or a pie in one's face. Moe, Larry, and Curly also spend a considerable amount of on-screen time destroying their own borrowed male uniforms, ripping up business suits, destroying top hats in myriad fashions, ripping one another's tuxedos. These repetitive acts of destruction of male class-drag clothing call attention to the fact that men's business and formal attire is indeed a rigid set of clothes that have "made the man," with very little variance, for centuries. The male business suit is a simple outfit that has changed very little over the years. Similarly, the clothes of the aristocrat, the wealthy man's tuxedo, is a "classic" outfit the design of which has changed little over time.

The top hat, white shirt, and the tailcoat seem timeless. Their stark black and white are a concretized visual reminder of the rigidity of codes of proper male behavior. This realization is why watching the Three Stooges, or Laurel and Hardy, or any number of comics destroy class-based male attire is pleasurable. They split their pants, they stomp on topcoats, they rip apart the business suit. Their destructive ways are not limited to their own clothes either. The gags often revolve around the "boys'" destruction of the clothes of real butlers, businessmen and businesswomen, matronly women of aristocratic bearing, and rich men in tuxedos. Wearing the business suit or a tux requires class entitlement and signifies either employment or idle wealth. It also signifies a willingness to play the corporate game and to believe in the reality of class. Ripping up suits and destroying tuxedos is so popular in male comedy that it works as a trope of empowerment of the disenfranchised. The Marx Brothers use the trope constantly to great effect. These boys do not want jobs; they reject class and the manhood that goes along with class privilege. This violence is one way to deal with a system one did not invent, one cannot beat, and one wishes to violently reject.

Like women, men are taught to envy others in American culture. In her study of envy in U.S. consumer society, *Keeping Up with the Joneses,* Susan J. Matt speaks to the issue of envy in men as it was manipulated in the 1920s.

> Although corporate leaders asked men to suppress their envy in the workplace, they were encouraged to act on the emotion in the marketplace. During the 1920s, American men were encouraged to repress their emotions at work, but they were given increasing opportunities for emotional release outside of it. Consumer spending on status goods represented a silent and less aggressive form of competition with coworkers and acquaintances. . . . Emotional repression at work and release outside of it benefited not only the corporations in search of office harmony, but also the companies that produced cars, office equipment, furniture, clothing, and countless other items that could be used for purposes of conspicuous display. . . .
>
> The widely held conviction that well-kept business clothes, stylish cars, and well-appointed offices were crucial to higher social status was symptomatic of the growing cultural emphasis on material goods as signals of success. By the late 1910s and 1920s, some commentators claimed that the desire to own class-marked objects was what motivated men to work. Men no longer struggled to win positions for the honor and prestige that they inherently possessed but for the buying power that they would grant. Success was no longer only or primarily evident in the job a man held but in what he owned and displayed. (90)

Men are taught to envy and be enviable as a mark of class mobility, driving a permanent wedge between men that acts as a capitalist tool to prevent them from forming alliances to disrupt labor and the marketplace. One thing that is mesmerizing about the Three Stooges, Laurel and Hardy, and the Marx Brothers is that while they may envy others, they stick together as friends regardless of the crazy plots they live out.

Perhaps no better example of mocking the expectations of maleness, class, and capitalism can be found than *Duck Soup* (Leo McCarey, 1933). In this anarchist, almost Dadaist gag fest, the plot centers on Groucho as the eccentric Rufus T. Firefly, who woos the millionairess Mrs. Teasdale (Margaret Dumont) for her money. Mrs. Teasdale insists that Firefly be made the dictator of the mythical country of Freedonia because she is convinced that only Firefly can save the nation from bankruptcy, a predictable Depression-era theme. Throughout the film, Groucho insults the wealthy and aristocratic Mrs. Teasdale, as well as the pompous ambassador of the neighboring country of Sylvania (Louis Calhern).

Duck Soup not only pulls the rug out from underneath the masquerade of maleness and class, it also takes great pains to make a mockery of war itself. War is typically troped as a masculine affair of heroism that can trump even class, but war is a complete sham in *Duck Soup*. Here war is not at all about male heroism. Instead, it is about side-switching, double-crossing absurd games between sham dictators who destroy their own countries. Many people saw the film as flying in the face of the rising fascist regimes in several countries. Mussolini famously banned the film in Italy.

The American Dream, ironically, alienates the male breadwinner from the family he helps to create and for whom he sacrifices to support. He is often portrayed as alienated from the private sphere of the family home. The W. C. Fields comedy *It's a Gift* (Norman McLeod, 1934) offers the viewer a ripe example of the alienated breadwinner. Here, Fields plays Harold Bissonette, a small-time businessman who owns his own business but is the victim of a nagging wife and horribly selfish children. Poor Harold is bitten by the bug of the American Dream: class mobility.

Dreams of the good life seem within Bissonette's grasp when he inherits enough money to buy a California orange grove, only to have it swindled away from him. Along the way, we are treated to innumerable examples of the alienated male breadwinner who is unable to relax, even in his own home. At one point, Harold is simply trying to get a good night's sleep. His family, a noisy milkman, a baby who obnoxiously pelts him with grapes, and a salesman constantly interrupt his sleep. The trope of the working male desperately trying to get a good night's sleep is rampant in American pop culture. Consequently, characters such as Stan and Ollie, Daffy Duck, Elmer Fudd, and countless male figures spend many sleepless nights.

Oddly, only the male figures are the ones who cannot get any sleep. This is a trope that is at once about the human condition but is also gendered and classed. If men can never get any sleep, neither can they get any rest. Poor Dagwood Bumstead! In both the comic strip and the *Blondie* movies based on the strip, Blondie, Dagwood's wife, constantly pesters him. Dagwood and Blondie are interesting also in their pursuit of class mobility—or lack thereof.

In the first of the twenty-eight-film series, *Blondie* (Frank Strayer, 1938), Dagwood Bumstead loses his job. He is too embarrassed to tell his wife, and his unusual behavior starts to seem like that of a philanderer. Naturally, Blondie thinks Dagwood is cheating on her. The next *Blondie* picture in the series, *Blondie Meets the Boss* (Frank Strayer, 1939), plays on the fear of women entering the public sphere and taking "men's jobs." When Dagwood goes on a fishing trip, Blondie takes over Dagwood's job, with predictably funny results.

By 1949 Dagwood is more comfortable with Blondie's ability to save the family. Blondie wins a radio quiz show and saves Dagwood from a lifetime of manual labor in *Blondie Hits the Jackpot* (Edward Bernds, 1949). Blondie proves herself more capable than her husband in achieving the American Dream of class mobility in several of the *Blondie* films. In *Blondie in the Dough* (Abby Berlin, 1947), Blondie goes into the baking business. Most *Blondie* movies, however, revolve around Dagwood getting into trouble with his boss, getting into trouble with his wife, or both. Dagwood is portrayed as lazy and often quite stupid. In recent years, the comic-strip version of *Blondie* has seen her open a successful catering business, while Dagwood remains stuck as a wage slave, continually capitulating to Mr. Dithers's tyrannical demands. Blondie, in short, wears the pants in the Bumstead family.

If anything, the Bumsteads are downwardly mobile. The *Blondie* films and comic strip remind men that attaining a job does not guarantee lifetime financial security. Katherine S. Newman writes in *Falling from Grace*,

> Attaining a responsible white-collar job, a skilled blue-collar job, or a stable marriage is no key to a lifetime of security. One can play by the rules, pay one's dues, and still be evicted from the American Dream.

There simply is no guarantee that one's best efforts will be rewarded in the end. . . .

And it is the violation of their older, more optimistic expectations, the uncovering of the naked truth about how precarious comfort is, that makes downward mobility so difficult for them to bear.

Feelings of anger or dismay, a sense of injustice—these are the responses to downward mobility shared by most of its victims. They worked hard for what they had, deferred gratification when necessary, and sacrificed when called upon by their country or their families. But the experience of downward mobility makes it abundantly clear that this is not enough. (229)

Implicit in the American Dream is the buried myth that all men are created equal as wage slaves. Women are supposed to be slaves to the family, of course. Naturally, I do not wish to pretend that these myths have not changed over time. Quite the contrary; these destructive myths are constantly being questioned, rehearsed, performed, and ruptured in American popular culture. But the myth remains that men, despite their class lineage, are born to be "men of action," to be "breadwinners," "inventors," always in pursuit of more things, more money, more at the office, more at the gym.

Maleness is about never having or being enough as consumers or class-passers. That's the American way of masculinity, especially straight masculinity. That explains the success of the television makeover program, *Queer Eye for the Straight Guy*, in which five gay men help a straight man to class-pass and perform his masculinity better. The fab five insist that it's not a makeover show but a "make-better" show, and indeed that is just what they do: they make one straight man appear better, although not through a massive makeover—no plastic surgery here. They help the straight man class-pass just enough so that he seems civilized.

Queer Eye for the Straight Guy is fascinating in terms of class and masculinity. Each show adheres to an absolutely strict formula. The viewer is repeatedly reminded that the fab five are simply trying to help the straight guy to "get to the next level," itself a measure of class mobility. Each show begins with the requisite tour of the straight man's home, usually associated with filth and beastliness; the "squalor" is noted; and the straight guy is taunted for being a "pig" whose abode is, in all fairness, that of an uncivilized slob.

Formulaic shots of a filthy shower, a disgusting toilet, and a heap of dirty clothes are almost always included, as are shots of the straight male body itself, filthy, poorly shaven or unshaven, stringy long hair or ill-fitting "rug." These men are usually fairly disgusting to the eye. Straight masculinity is associated with dirt, earth, smells ("You can just smell through the lens"), and brutishness. Men have always been associated with beastliness; think of old movies in which sexually predatory males are referred to as "wolves" and "hound dogs." Men cannot very well class-pass if they are not even considered human. To achieve the level of being human, the straight male needs to learn how to clean up his apartment; tame his hairy, unkempt body; and learn basic cooking and etiquette skills. He needs these abilities to class-pass, and the *Queer Eye* fab five offer them to him. For years, men had to rely on either parenting or etiquette books to help them in pursuing upward mobility. As I wrote in 2000 in a study of etiquette books, *Troping the Body,*

> etiquette books by male authors provide an elaborate map to men's social desires and goals within the patriarchal world. The authors of these texts accept the diametric opposition between the feminine and the masculine, a "them versus us" strategy that leads to an (unnatural) separation of men and women and the separate spheres of female/private and male/public interests. Accordingly, the main selling points of etiquette books for men is the promise of an increase of social confidence and economic gain in the public sphere through manners. The grotesque body of the male is troped as a fiscal commodity, denied individuality, and constrained physically. (11)

Jack Boozer identifies a category of films about men who fail at class mobility in the public sphere. In *Career Movies,* Boozer dubs this type of movie "the rise-and-fall overreacher film." In this category are several 1950s films, including *The Sweet Smell of Success* (Alexander MacKendrick, 1957) and *A Face in the Crowd* (Elia Kazan, 1957). Men are expected to call on their beastliness to be upwardly mobile and succeed in the aptly named "urban jungle" of the corporate world. These same supposed "instincts" of masculinity that they must shed to have good manners are often called on in the interest of passing as successful businessmen.

The Sweet Smell of Success offers us two examples of men who perform masculinity with vicious bravado. Sidney Falco, played by Tony Curtis, is a sleazy Broadway manager who desperately needs publicity for his clients. Thus he becomes dependent on J. J. Hunsecker (played by Burt Lancaster), a brutally successful syndicated newspaper columnist, loosely based on tabloid veteran Walter Winchell. The attitude toward ambition in the film is disgust. Here is a film noir in which male class-passing is associated with darkness and the grime of a neon-lit urbanscape that houses the corrupt and encourages overreaching. Lancaster's performance is magnificent. He plays the columnist as repressed, manic, controlling, and forbidding. The backdrop of New York allows him to portray a vicious beast in well-tailored suits with well-tailored manners in swanky nightclubs and trendy upscale nightspots. Curtis is also brilliant in his role as the overreacher. He is the class-passer who cannot quite rise above his station, largely because of the manner in which he speaks. His Brooklyn accent is a distinct liability.

As Emily Post wrote in 1945, "a man whose social position is self-made is likely to be detested" (588). Speech is a marker of good "breeding" and education, neither of which Sidney Falco has been privileged to have. Post's words about the cultivation of eloquent and charming speech are telling.

> No speaker who searches for words is interesting. Beautiful speech is like a brook that ripples on and on. Irritating speech is like the puffing of a locomotive, each puff broken with er-er—and-er, the listeners sharing in the search and also sharing in the effort with which each word is pronounced. (39)

Falco is a fast-talking, loud, irritating speaker. He uses speech to steamroller others in his desperate attempt to achieve success. But Hunsecker is articulate, well spoken, even smarmy. He is especially smarmy when speaking quietly, setting up a poor young man, Steve Dallas (played by Martin Milner), for a crime he did not commit. Hunsecker is jealous of Dallas because the young man is romantically involved with Hunsecker's sister, Susan (played by Susan Harrison). Hunsecker has incestuous feelings for Susan, who lives with him in an odd familial arrangement. The film seems to associate American male overreaching with Hunsecker's indeterminate sexuality and his obsession with his own sister.

Hunsecker asks Falco to break up Susan's romance with Dallas, a jazz musician, by planting some marijuana in Dallas's topcoat pocket and tipping off the cops. In return, Hunsecker offers Falco plenty of publicity in his column. When Falco becomes mixed up with Hunsecker's thugs, Hunsecker eventually ruins him. Eventually both characters are destroyed because of their inability to play by the rules of the American Dream. Falco's chicanery is matched by Hunsecker's velvet-gloved thuggery. This film noir suggests that men, no matter what their class, are beasts after all, even if they are beasts in topcoats.

A Face in the Crowd also trades on the ideology of man-beast as failed class-passer. Andy Griffith plays a small-town huckster and singer, Lonesome Rhodes, in an absolutely stellar performance. Patricia Neal plays Marcia Jeffries, a driven young woman who puts Lonesome Rhodes on her local television station in Arkansas. Rhodes, encouraged by his newfound fame, begins doling out homespun wit and backwater stories. Soon he is drawing the largest audience of any network program. He believes his own publicity and becomes a megalomaniac who mistreats everyone around him, becoming increasingly reckless as his ambition grows. He becomes truly terrifying and begins to have political aspirations.

Meant as a scathing critique of the wages of the sins of capitalism, *A Face in the Crowd* warns the classed against taking in the unclassed. Ultimately unable to class-pass, the poor, white-trash figure is a dangerous, beastly arrogant hillbilly who cannot be tamed. Lower-class men are often such beasts who cannot be tamed, even by the class system and soul-crushing capitalist ideology.

Fredric March plays an overreacher in the classic vehicle about corporate class-passing, *Executive Suite* (Robert Wise, 1954). Written by Ernest Lehman and based on the novel by Cameron Hawley, the film revolves around the death of a corporate president and the power jockeying that ensues among several executives who attempt to claw their way to the vacated top spot.

March's portrayal of Loren Phineas Shaw is much like the brilliant and over-the-top performances of Andy Griffith in *A Face in the Crowd* and Burt Lancaster in *The Sweet Smell of Success*. Masculinity and mobility are intertwined with obsessive and villainous behavior. Nothing can stop Shaw's driving force. He must win at all costs, even while insisting that his behavior is driven only by good business sense and rationality. In contrast, William Holden plays McDonald Walling, the more beneficent character who wishes to pursue the American Dream but harbors a sense of fairness and decency that holds him back.

In 1987 Oliver Stone made *Wall Street*, a film in many ways reminiscent of *Executive Suite*. Michael Douglas plays Gordon Gekko and Charlie Sheen is Bud Fox, a young executive who wishes to make $1 million. Morality again tempers class rise when Fox is successfully tempted to take a job with the crooked and lecherous corporate takeover artist Gekko. Class again emerges as a significant—if often overlooked—plot hook when Bud Fox, who is from a working-class family, uses information he learns from his father Carl (played by Martin Sheen) about the airline his father works for. Class-passing and the temptation of class mobility are at the center of the moral question of the film's pivotal character, Bud Fox.

I think the choice of the name "Bud Fox" is interesting because it makes us think of a budding fox, a fox in the making, an animal in the making. Gordon Gekko is seen as a shark. Using these animalistic names and metaphors when we talk about corporate greed again brings us into a discussion of the trope of men as predatory animals. *Wall Street* was made just before the "go-go" 1990s, the decade in which we saw the rise of corporate takeovers.

In early 2004 the Fox network presented the absurd spectacle of *Man vs. Beast II*, in which men "compete" with animals, which strikes me as an utterly absurd concept but one in keeping with the ideology of male beastliness, Darwinian corporate ideology, and the myth of successful male class mobility. The most bizarre aspect of the show is that animals can hardly compete with humans if they have no way of knowing that they are indeed "competing." In one such competition, an Olympic athlete tries to outlast a chimpanzee in a contest that involves hanging from a bar. The chimpanzee "loses" when he goes against the rules by putting his feet against a side rail.

Anyone watching the program can determine that the chimpanzee could certainly hang longer than any human. Another section features a tree-climbing "competition" between a Samoan man who regularly climbs trees competitively and a bear who, again, does not really know he is competing. Finally, in a ghastly and embarrassing spectacle, a team of little people runs a race with a camel. The program must receive good ratings because it is on Fox; any show that does not perform immediately in the ratings war is unceremoniously dropped from its programming lineup. How can we possibly understand the fascination of bringing humans and beasts together and trying to entertain the public with their "competition"? Perhaps the Fox producers are simply recalling turn-of-the-century sideshows, but more likely they are responding to some sort of cultural need to reinject masculinity with beastliness.

As a female viewer, I feel I can only postulate wildly. As a cultural critic, I'm tempted to say that Fox's *Man vs. Beast II*, like *Survivor, Fear Factor,* and the antics of performance artist and masochist David Blaine, are attempts to reestablish the masculine domain in the area of action, pain, and physicality. As always, male consumers are subject to multiple and conflicting messages about masculinity and the American Dream of luxury, idleness, and prosperity. The idealization of men of action in the media suggests a relationship between class-passing and masculinity that is impossible to unravel. Take for example the blatant and repetitive icons of men who have been successful in achieving the American Dream.

I find something quite pathetic and desperate about Donald Trump's appearance in the reality television show *The Apprentice*. Apparently, Trump can never get enough recognition. Buildings in New York and Atlantic City sport his name, and countless television shows and print media have covered his rise and fall and comeback. Enough Donald Trump already. And how do we account for the numerous lengthy written and televised profiles of class-passers of notable achievement, such as Warren Buffet, Bill Gates, Michael Eisner, P. Diddy, Richard Branson, and Miramax's Weinstein brothers? MTV's *Cribs* offers us the spectacle of numerous celebrities who have successfully achieved the American Dream, and yet seemingly never can enough be done to recognize that achievement.

Does not the endless pursuit of publicity inherently undermine their achievement? Or do the audiences, desperate to cling to the American Dream, need constantly to see images of those who have successfully class-passed, along with the trophies of class-passing: the cars, the "cribs," the women, the yachts, the private planes, the clothes closets, the pools, the bodyguards, the private weight trainer, the many servants, and all that heaven does not allow the common man or woman?

Look at the February 2004 issue of the *Robb Report,* a magazine dedicated to upwardly mobile and rich men's fantasies. The pullout subscription card advertises the magazine as "what makes the good life great!" as if the reader might not quite have a clue as to how to live the good life, even if given a chance. Looking at the *Robb Report* is a peek inside corporate culture as it tries to sell its products to corporate culture. The front cover sports numerous shiny new cars outside a massive building and fronted by a spectacular fountain.

What's interesting here is the lack of any human beings in the photograph. No footprints appear in the sand around the cars. No people appear in the majority of the ads and the photo spreads—only products such as the Infinity Q45, which "packs 340 horsepower but still spoils you with everything" (1). The Richard Mille wristwatch from Westime, described as "a racing machine on the wrist," is presented in another ad devoid of humanity (2–3). Next is a two-page ad for Exclusive Resorts that features vacation spots largely devoid of people. On the left is a beautiful shot of a beach from the point of view of a chaise longue on which rests a woman's straw hat and a towel. Where have all the people gone? On the right page are four photos of luxury properties. One shot shows a pool in a magisterial courtyard. Underneath that shot is a photo of a cozy-looking interior of a cabin in Telluride, Colorado, with, again, no people. A shot of the interior of an exclusive motel in downtown San Francisco sits under Telluride. Finally, the bottom photo shows a glimpse of a human being sitting in a beach chair in the background at a resort in Scottsdale, Arizona. Prominent in the ad is the copy, which reads "an invitation to the most exclusive club on earth" (4–5). Exclusive? This club is apparently so exclusive that one is not likely to run into any people at its "residences."

Subsequent pages have additional ads that have no people in them, such as the ad for Cohiba cigars (6–7). The ad on the following pages features a driver-free Hummer (8–9). Finally, six pages into the magazine, the first human to actually look at us in the magazine, a woman emerging from a pool used to hawk Beaudry diamonds in a two-page spread: "Always in My Dreams" (10–11). Luxury items are pitched at the affluent, and the woman who emerges from the water is not quite human. She is only a dream acquisition after all, and from the looks of the ad, it looks as though her price is expensive: no less than three huge, gaudy diamond rings center the photo, and a dazzling, diamond-encrusted locket is dangled, Maya Deren–style, into the frame.

Apparently, when the ad copy says "exclusivity," it really means *no one* is invited. Of 144 pages, I counted no fewer than 130 that included no people, no traces of people: empty couches, driverless cars, resorts that have apparently undergone some sort of end-of-days rapture scenario, an endless catalog of empty luxury cars, even a luxury airline without any of those pesky pilots or crew to mess up the airbrushed photographs. Is all this sterility meant to suggest that so much class privilege exists that class mobility is beyond the reach of *any* human hand? Thinking perhaps that my one depeopled issue of the *Robb Report* might be an anomaly, I took a look at the *Robb Report Collection* (February 2004) and found, again, a panoply of luxury items and few people. The only shot dominated by a bodily figure that I could find was an ad for Michael Jordan's Senior Flight School (54), a fantasy basketball camp for upwardly mobile suburbanites with a requisite shot of Mr. Jordan. Otherwise, I found empty mansions, living rooms, ships, islands, golf courses, and more luxury charter airlines, eerily manned by no one.

The effect is frightening and reminiscent of the beginning of the British science-fiction classic *Village of the Damned* (Wolf Rilla, 1960), in which aliens put a whole town to sleep and mysteriously impregnate all the village women with alien children of a sort of Aryan superrace, origin unknown. The *Robb Report* and the *Robb Report Collection* let us know that a frighteningly powerful, elite, rich club into which most of us are definitely and emphatically not invited does indeed exist.

This thought brings me to the impossibility of full class-passing and class mobility in American culture. Even those at the very top of the political spectrum are subject to the rules of class-passing. Bill Clinton did a really poor job of class-passing. He deliberately chose to "slum" and to pretend not to embrace the near-royalty we bequeath to our presidents and their first ladies. His presidency, his actions, and those of his family continually were called into question. The same working-class Arkansas roots that helped to elect Clinton were the same roots regarded as examples of hick behavior, and an intrinsically lower class marked him and his presidency.

Similarly, George W. Bush, even though born into a wealthy privileged family, can never fully class-pass, mainly because he cannot speak well. He has become famous for his faltering, mind-numbingly amazing misuse of the English language. He is fraudulent as a class-passer, and his speech reflects poorly on his actions and presidency. Oddly enough, he has managed to become popular with the ignorant masses, who perhaps share his inability to speak the King's English. I cannot help but pass along some advice from Emily Post to George W. Bush.

> There is no better way to cultivate a perfect pronunciation, apart from association with cultivated people, than by getting a small pronouncing dictionary of words in ordinary use, and reading it word by word, marking and studying any that you use frequently and mispronounce. When you know them, read any book at random slowly aloud to yourself, very carefully pronouncing each word.
>
> You should, moreover, look up in a dictionary every word you meet that you do not thoroughly know. Another convenient way to enlarge your vocabulary as well as to correct your faults of pronunciation is that of a notable lawyer, whose early advantages had not taught him good English, but who won a high reputation for the purity of his speech. The secret of his achievement was that for years he wrote words or phrases, a few at a time, on his bathroom mirror with soap! Then he practiced these words by saying them over and over to himself, day after day, while he shaved and dressed. Later on, when these words were thoroughly fixed in his mind, other words were written in their place. The consciousness of these exercises may make you stilted in conversa-

tion at first, but by and by the "sense" or "impulse" to speak correctly will come.

This is a method that has been followed by many men handicapped in youth through lack of education, who have become prominent in public life, and by many women who, likewise handicapped by circumstances, have not only made possible a creditable position for themselves, but have then given their children the inestimable advantage of learning their mother tongue correctly at their mother's knee. (39)

When I look though the landscape of popular film, I expect to find plenty of narratives that encourage men to seek control of money and the class mobility that goes along with money. Instead I find narratives that punish the executive and hated on-screen male figures, often played by Warren William. That William played so many "heavies" during the pre-Code years of the 1930s is ironic because he was not particularly ambitious in real life. In fact, he was utterly lazy. In Mick LaSalle's study of pre-Code men and modernity, *Dangerous Men*, LaSalle notes that William was so lazy that "he invented an apartment on wheels—the 1930s equivalent of a Winnebago—so he could shower and get made up on the way to the studio" (151).

William played ruthless ambitious tycoons and scoundrels in classic films such as Howard Bretherton and William Keighley's *The Match King* (1932), Roy del Ruth's *Employees' Entrance* (1933), and Edgar Selwyn's *Skyscraper Souls* (1932). William's on-screen career is quite interesting, given that maternal melodramas were punishing women for attempts at class-passing at the same moment in film history. Warren William's class-passing is also frequently punished or at least cast in a harsh light. Nevertheless, audiences could take away their own perceptions and receptions of pleasure and identification with William's heels, robber barons, gangsters, and overly zealous tycoons.

As Mick LaSalle notes, Warren William was "the ultimate scoundrel lover . . . the ultimate fixer, the ultimate liar, the ultimate manipulator" (149). Although almost completely forgotten today, he was once a huge box-office draw. Appearing in some of the best pre-Code films between 1932 and 1935, William was a tall version of John Barrymore who specialized in playing rats, crooks, and villains. In Roy del Ruth's *The Mind Reader* (1933), William passes himself off as a psychic named Chandra the Great. He takes advantage of the virginal white Constance Cummings. *The Mind Reader* typifies a Warren William performance: oily, oozing with charm, able to pass himself off as a class act. In *Skyscraper Souls*, his character is the modernism-embracing visionary who wishes to build the world's tallest skyscraper.

Skyscraper Souls, based on the Faith Baldwin novel, includes scenes of William as the ultimate American corporate huckster, motivated by greed and with a firm belief in the myth of the American Dream. His character, David Dwight, manipulates stock prices and is as ruthless in the bedroom as he is in the boardroom. He throws over his loyal secretary, Verree Teasdale, for a younger woman at the office, the pale virginal white Maureen O'Sullivan (known for her performance as Jane in *Tarzan the Ape Man* of the same year). But he goes too far when he cheats on the fragile young woman, who then shoots him and jumps off the top of his enormous skyscraper.

In *The Match King,* perhaps William's most telling example of class-passing, he portrays an unscrupulous young man who becomes a millionaire by craftily buying up the rights to all match-manufacturing machines throughout the world. It is a mean-spirited Horatio Alger tale and a fictionalized biography of real-life businessman Ivar Kreuger. In the film he is called Paul Kroll, and he starts as an immigrant doing janitorial work at a baseball stadium in Chicago. He helps his boss in a scheme to rob the employees, and then he robs his boss and flees to Sweden.

His class-passing begins in Sweden. Kroll lies to his parents and convinces them that he's a successful American businessman with vast wealth in the United States. His parents believe his lies and give him control of their matchmaking business. Kroll then manages to gain control, one by one, of all the other matchmaking plants in Europe. He's a cruel character who will stop at nothing. His favorite phrase to placate his unsuspecting victims is "just leave everything to me," implying that he will look after his competitor's interests. Nothing could be further from Kroll's actual intentions. When a poor, eccentric inventor comes up with a reusable match that could ruin Kroll's empire, Kroll destroys the man and manages to have him thrown into an insane asylum. Along the way, Kroll seduces and abandons countless women. He is such a thoroughgoing rat that he is fun to watch. William gave Depression-era audiences a fantasy figure who moved up in the world. Is it a twisted send-up of the American Dream, or does it actually capture the dream's inherent evil? For audiences, it demonstrated that a street sweeper could indeed create an empire through sheer will and a lack of moral fiber.

William's next film featured a character similar to that of Ivar Kreuger. *Employees' Entrance* features William as Kurt Anderson, the lecherous and ruthless manager of an American department store. People are always jumping out windows in Warren William films, and *Employees' Entrance* is no exception. Desperate to keep his department store afloat during the Great Depression, Anderson presses his top executives for fresh marketing ideas. An older executive disagrees timidly, and Anderson fires him on the spot. Later, when Anderson hears that the same man committed suicide by jumping out a window, Anderson coldly announces, "When a man outlives his usefulness, he ought to jump out of a window." Anderson date-rapes a hungry young woman (played by Loretta Young) he picks up on the street. He gets her drunk at an office party, brings her to his apartment upstairs, and leaves, but returns and takes advantage of the young woman's inebriation.

William class-passes again in Robert Florey's *Bedside* (1934). In this film he plays a drunk who manages to obtain a fake diploma as a medical doctor. He performs surgery on an opera singer and almost kills her. Amazingly, he seeks out publicity; he likes to see himself mentioned by the gossip columnists. He's a thoroughgoing cad who becomes a doctor to the celebrities with whom he ingratiates himself. As Mick LaSalle concludes, the film's message is loud and clear: "Lack of morals, lack of ethics, lack of honest application, and a lack of wholesome personal habits present no obstacle to success in America" (160).

The myth of the corporate male "rat" is part of the fabric of the American Dream, in which class mobility must be achieved at any price. Men are seen as having to take drastic measures to get ahead, so the end seemingly justifies *any* means. Gangster films of the era provide excellent examples. *Scarface* (Howard Hawks, 1932), *The Public Enemy* (William Wellman, 1931), and *Little Caesar* (Mervyn LeRoy, 1930) are all classic gangster films that embrace violence as a means to achieve social mobility in the United States. Thomas Doherty notes of *Scarface* that "the imagery and backstory of F. Scott Fitzgerald's *The Great Gatsby* informs Ben Hecht's literate script, the sense that the fresh green beast of the New World has rotted on the vine, the cultural memory of 1925 having become the economic report of 1932" (148).

Gangsters have made a measurable comeback of late, and gangsters and thugs, both black and white, watch and fetishize the images of class-passing gangster films of the 1930s, as well as the more recent versions of *Scarface* and the television series *The Sopranos*. Gangsta thuggery could not be more popular, both in and out of rap culture. Gangsta rap provides a "ghetto pass" to white youngsters looking for role models. The Horatio Alger myth has become one of class-passing at any cost. Violence is no longer seen as a sad side effect of class rise. It is not just a means to an end. Violence has always been embedded in the American Dream.

Although the pacific-looking ads in the *Robb Report* seem to endorse consumer worship of calm, depeopled spaces devoid of violence, a closer look exposes the barely suppressed celebration of violence that sells the priceless objects of desire. Take the cover story "*Robb Report*'s Car of the Year 2004," for example. Paul Dean's report is rife with samples of the violence and carnage inherently possible in this year's most desirable automobiles. At number one, the Bentley Continental GT is offered as "an ungoverned, 198 mph Supercar" (63). When you look at the car, you'll "see power and purpose . . . broad haunches and a strong serious face. [It] is to sense pure animal attraction" (63). For all of its animal attractions, the Bentley Continental GT, Dean assures us, is a secure vehicle: "I can think of no other high-performance vehicle that delivers this amount of security at [this] speed and this level of distinction" (63). In a related story on the Porsche 911 Turbo Cabriolet, Fluto Shinzawa reminds us that safety is not an important priority but speed and ballistic capability are: "The Cabriolet is my runaway favorite. It has the acceleration of a cannonball. It relishes long-distance cruising as well as short, frenzied blasts" (quoted in R. Ross 69).

The advertised cars exude the promise of violent death as a form of mobility, perhaps the ultimate mobility beyond class, beyond the body, the true American Dream. Mikita Brottman considers the American love affair with car crashes in *Car Crash Culture,* noting,

> In the United States in particular—historically, a restless, mobile society—the automobile has always been the most obvious index of individual prosperity and personal control. But America's wonder and worship at the glory of the automobile as a totem of change, speed, and technological progress has a grim underside. No other civilian invention has such an enormous degree of carnage associated with its everyday use. Unlike Europe, much of the United States was constructed with the automobile in mind. Consequently, the car has become as iconic to U.S. culture as the gun. If the automobile signifies wealth, movement, progress, and all that is venerated in America, then vehicular death embodies its counterpart—that violent rage toward destruction that lies beneath the surface of the proverbial "pioneer spirit." (xxxvi)

Other ads present themselves as crime scenes photographed before the violence ensues. An ad for Ca'd'Oro, the Jewel at the Venetian, a luxury jewelry store at the Venetian Hotel in Las Vegas, looks very much like a set for a burglary about to happen (101). Something is inherently violent about the noirish lighting and set design. The glass cases implore the viewer to imagine themselves smashing their glass and grasping their expensive fortunes. An ad for Land Rover looks as if the vehicle has come to a halt after a lengthy filmed chase scene, the vehicle parked inexplicably beneath two overpasses of the type used in most chase scenes (17). Perhaps it has just landed from a forty-foot drop. As if that were not enough promise of violence and action, a story on state-of-the-art audio systems promises "thermionic extremism" with "driving enormous single-driver horn speakers" (Fisher 51). An ad for the Dodge Charger Daytona promises the near-death experience of NASCAR racing.

> Cheatin' has long been a way of life in NASCAR racing, so it was inevitable that the car manufacturers would get into it. Ford, Chrysler, and General Motors—the latter officially uninterested in the sport—first came up with special engines. These were often installed in cars never offered to the public. Then Chrysler upped the ante with the droop-snoot, bewinged Dodge Charger Daytona and its near-twin, the Plymouth Superbird. Even though ordinary folks could buy them (if they tried hard enough), these aerodynamic, Hemi-powered brutes were meant to win races. And they did—so successfully that they were effectively banned from competition in 1971 (18–19).

Apparently we should desire certain death along with our secure depeopled luxury lifestyle, at least according to the images and text in the *Robb Report*.

Our thirst for violence knows no boundaries and is inexplicably related to our conflicting notions of the American Dream. The images of desire in popular culture are meant to bridge the contradictions in capitalist consumer ideals. Material success, regardless of the way it is defined or distorted, is more worthy as a goal than as a result, which of course leads to satiation or disillusionment. We discover our identity as we interrogate our desires. Commodity and exchange values become abstracted, as do identity and desire. Untangling the myths of class mobility from this heterogeneous mix of ideas, ideologies, and images becomes impossible when people identify with what they consume rather than with what they produce.

Celebrity Fantasies: Marriage and Class Mobility

$\mathbf{T}$he power of images to isolate and promote some fantasies while suppressing and repressing other fantasies and realities works toward *déclassement*, or down-classing. While our dreams of celebrity are fed continually, we all die a little and suppress more than a little reality. "Reality" programs should really be called "fantasy," whereas, ironically, fictional dramas sometimes do the nasty work of reminding us about class reality, unemployment, and massive debt. The average family in the United States owes, according to recent statistics, $18,654 per household in unsecured debt, not including mortgage debts (Khan). Moreover, as Kim Khan notes,

> about 43% of American families spend more than they earn each year. Average households carry some $8,000 in credit card debt. Personal bankruptcies have doubled in the past decade. . . . American consumers owed a grand total of $1.9733 trillion in October 2003, according to the latest statistics on consumer credit from the Federal Reserve. That's about $18,654 per household, a figure that doesn't include mortgage debt. The number is up more than 41% from the $1.3999 trillion consumers owed in 1998. . . . The majority of consumer borrowing, about 53%, is represented by so-called "non-revolving" debt such as

automobile loans. But "revolving" credit, which most typically involves credit cards, is an increasingly significant part of the equation. Revolving debt currently totals $735.3 billion; that's about 31% higher than it was only five years ago. The figure has more than doubled in a decade. . . . [Indeed,] the most recent Federal Reserve study showed that 43% of U.S. families spent more than they earned. On average, Americans spend $1.22 for each dollar they earn. (screens 1, 2)

Despite this debt, and perhaps even because of the expected downsizing of the average American, we are inundated with fetishistic displays of celebrity, or at least what passes as celebrity in popular culture. The list of reality programs with the word *celebrity* in the title is seemingly unending, from *Celebrity Weddings* to *Celebrity Breakups*. These programs mark a wave of almost pornographic indecency in terms of their celebration of ostentatious wealth. They run alongside a parade of programs that ask *Who Wants to Be a Millionaire?*, *How Stars Got Hot,* and why *It's Good to Be Britney Spears,* for example.

In a fascinating discussion of the perils of the class structure, William E. Connolly notes that we must "engage the problem of evil residing within human structures of personal identity and social order" because isn't taunting us all with such conflicting images concerning class and wealth implicitly evil (3)? A subversive yet fascist machine is working to conceal the threats to the American Dream in favor of a pack of lies that distort our very own fantasies, our very own visions of our selves, and our own ownership of our bodies, all in an effort to move us to purchase more and believe that we are just like celebrities, with very little reality in the way of our own identification and becoming one with celebrity.

The current cultural schizophrenia is like any other mass hysteria in that stepping away from the machinery to see the insanity is difficult. But, as Connolly warns,

> every culture seems to contain some themes that are both indispensable to it and inherently problematic within it. The pressure of their indispensability works to conceal their problematic character. This sometimes becomes clear retrospectively after the indispensability of a theme has been lost or compromised; then *aporias* within it flood into the open, making contemporaries wonder how their forerunners could ever have entertained such superstitious or absurd ideas. (3)

Our current climate of the cult of celebrity and our worship of the fetishized items associated with massive wealth seem to parallel the

Depression-era 1930s. However, in the 1930s the celebration and ritualized display of wealth and the wealthy were tempered to a great degree
by political awareness, the activity of union organizers and labor, and the
output of socially aware films. Mostly from Warner Brothers, these films
dealt with hardship and poverty. An example is William Wellman's *Wild
Boys of the Road* (1933), a film in which unemployed poverty-stricken
youths are forced to ride the rails during the Great Depression. Sure, the
media lied then, continually promising that "prosperity is just around the
corner," but those times differ from our times in that there were at least
a recognition of reality and opportunities for dissent.

We have witnessed a massive economic downturn, yet we tiptoe around
the words we use to describe it. The term *depression* is never used to describe the current economic climate; the term *economic downturn* seems
just euphemistic enough. People seem to think that because we no longer
have bread lines, so to speak, we are no longer in economic failure. What
is more likely, however, is that we as a culture are less caring and that the
reason we no longer have bread lines is that we no longer care enough to
enact a comprehensive and compassionate approach to those who are poverty-stricken.

The poor are Othered as deviants; their *déclassement* is seen as de-
served. Besides, we chase the illusion of wealth in our all-out embrace of
the credit card as the answer to money problems, and relatively few people
cannot obtain such a card. But credit, Pierre Bourdieu writes, "allows the
immediate enjoyment of the promised goods but implies acceptance of a
future, which is merely the continuation of the past, or the 'imitation'—
mock luxury cars, mock luxury holidays and so on" (164).

We are susceptible to not only the lure of class-passing with a credit
card but also the more massive and dangerous class-passing that goes with
it, from cars and vacations we cannot really afford to the *Lifestyles of the
Rich and Famous*. Lest we see through the charade of class-passing by
means of spending, we are continually reminded that it is okay to spend,
spend, spend.

When Virginia Heffernan interviewed David Chase, the creator of *The
Sopranos*, for the *New York Times*, he opined that "television is the base
of a lot of our problems" (20). Fed up with television, Chase declares,
"The function of an hour drama is to reassure the American people that
it's O.K. to go out and buy stuff. It's all about flattering the audience,
making them feel as if all the authority figures have our best interests at
heart" (1).

A typical episode of VH1's *The Fabulous Life: Celebrity Super Spenders* concentrates on the spending habits of Christina Aguilera, a recording "artist" who is perhaps more notable for her wearing underwear as outerwear than for her actual record sales. Nevertheless, a narrator who sounds distinctly like Robin Leach assures us that Aguilera can afford to spend to the point of wretched excess. "She's made $18 million in album sales, but that's before the $32 million she's made from concert performances." Lest we worry that Ms. Aguilera has any financial woes, we are reminded that she also makes many more millions in endorsements. "Her edgy sex appeal" has garnered her contracts with Coke and Sketchers.

During *The Fabulous Life* episode, we glimpse the celebrity walk-in closet, we gawk at the glamorous and spendthrift lifestyle of Aguilera, who "wouldn't even set foot outside without at least $2.5 million worth of bling on." Bling and ice, jewelry, is an important fetish item to the newly wealthy. At the end of the program, we learn that Aguilera is a philanthropist. The narrator duly notes that she gives to an organization for the blind, another charitable organization for wildlife preservation, and, perhaps most telling, an organization that works against domestic violence. What the narrator fails to mention is what any accountant knows. Celebrities do not give as individuals; they give as corporations and take a huge tax break for it.

The rags-to-riches story is alive and well and part of the fabric of the American Dream as it is refashioned around the cult of celebrity. E! Entertainment Television currently offers a series called *It's Good to Be . . .* (fill in the celebrity of the moment). Typical episodes include "Britney Spears's journey takes her from shy Southern girl to successful diva," "The worldwide celebrity of Paris and Nicky Hilton," and "The financial life of teen stars Mary Kate and Ashley Olsen." We now may know even more about the finances of the celebrities we worship than we do about our own financial portfolios. As Social Security is threatened, financial portfolios collapse, and greedy corporate magnates fleece retirement accounts, we are subject to a pornographic exhibition of the wealth and privilege of celebrity.

Throughout popular culture, we are repeatedly told that we are just like the rich, just like stars and celebrities, and they are just like us. A typical example is Sarah Tomczak's article in *US Weekly,* "Stars—They're Just Like Us!" "They shovel food in their mouths!" is the caption next to a photo of Lara Flynn Boyle scarfing down some falafel at the Beverly Glen deli in Los Angeles (24). "They refuel at Starbucks!" shrieks another caption for a photo of Angelina Jolie carrying a cardboard cup of Starbucks coffee (24). "They hunt for the right pair of jeans!" accompanies a photo of "jean queen Tori Spelling" as she shops for denim (25). "They have family reunions!" (25) sits above a photograph of Liv and Steven Tyler surrounded by family members.

The March 1, 2004, issue of *In Touch Weekly* has an almost identical article, "So Real—In Touch with Their Real Sides!" No author is credited with the captions and copy that accompany the photo spread here, which includes Ashton Kutcher, keeping it real with Demi Moore.

> What a gentleman! No, it's not a man-purse. Ashton Kutcher proves he loves Demi Moore enough to carry her bag, no matter what his buddies might say. As they left a get-together at a friend's house, the *Butterfly Effect* hunk refused to let his "old lady" shoulder the burden of books *and* a heavy bag. Ashton just turned 26, narrowing their age difference to only 15 years. (93)

Alongside photos of Reese Witherspoon and Camryn Manheim, we learn that celebrities are, just like us, proud of their children.

> They're proud moms. It may not be the *Mona Lisa,* but Reese Witherspoon couldn't be happier with 4-year-old daughter Ava's artwork. She beamingly flashed the preschooler's drawing while leaving her school. Meanwhile, Camryn Manheim shows that sometimes a kid's photo can be the best red-carpet accessory: At the premiere of the . . . Gene Hackman/Ray Romano movie, *Welcome to Mooseport,* Camryn brandished a pic of the main man in her life, her adorable 2-year-old son, Milo. Check out their matching smiles! (92)

Yes, they are keeping it real, just as Jennifer Lopez is still "Jenny from the Block," as she insists in her wildly successful hit pop song. We are just like you and you can class-pass as a celebrity is the not-so-secret message of the media. If you think celebrities don't have problems, watch VH1's *Celebrity Breakups,* part 2, which covers the romantic woes of Sharon Stone, Jude Law, Edward Norton, and Ashton Kutcher. If you think celebrities have no family secrets, wrong again! Watch Court TV's *Dominick Dunne: Power, Privilege and Justice.* See the special episode "Family Secrets," which reveals how a "miserly Salt Lake City millionaire is shot to death." We can find plenty of images of celebrities being caught by the law or at least finding themselves entangled with the law. NBC offers *Celebrity Justice* and Court TV offers *Hollywood Justice,* but both programs cover the same territory. The fascination with celebrities and their crimes is seemingly as bottomless as our desire to see celebrities get punished. In the past year, thousands of hours of television were dedicated to the Michael Jackson child-abuse allegations, as well as to the Martha Stewart insider-trading scandal and her trial. Now that she has actually been convicted of some of the charges, perhaps the networks and cable producers will cover the really big players in corporate fraud, but that is highly doubtful. Indeed, Martha Stewart's high media visibility has done her the most damage. She tried to class-pass but ultimately failed. As columnist Sheryl McCarthy astutely commented, "arrogance cooked Martha's goose," adding that

> . . . Stewart had built an empire by doing things just so, and was accustomed to having things her way. She must have thought she could have it in this instance too. There was also evidence of greed. The wealthy, we have learned from other divas like Leona Helmsley, are often quite penurious, seeking to claim every dime, to gain every advantage. Perhaps that's what gets them to their station in life. Stewart, we learned during the trial, billed her media company for tens of thousands of dollars for a personal vacation, when she could easily have paid for it herself. She was also used to enjoying advantages that ordinary folks don't have. Confiding to a pal that she'd received some confidential information about her ImClone stock, she allegedly said, "Isn't it nice to have brokers who tell you those things?"—or some words to that effect.

Clearly, we have more fun pillorying celebrities than unknowns. What do we know about the men who routinely raided our pensions, manipulated our country into wars for oil profit, and committed bank fraud? These men have managed to elude the spotlight, and they are therefore fairly uninteresting to a celebrity culture. But in the United States, as the late celebrity lawyer Johnnie Cochran often said, "you are innocent until *proven broke*" (Cochran's emphasis). Celebrities seldom end up doing any serious jail time but the possibility that they could keeps us watching and fuels the late-night comics with celebrity jokes.

We are flooded with images of products we are supposed to desire, products that we can ill afford, but in the new American Dream (no, nightmare) we are repeatedly told that we can afford the same fetishized products that the celebrities embody. We can afford the Manolo Blahnik shoes that Sarah Jessica Parker sports in real life—and on the recently concluded series *Sex and the City.* The assumption that we actually desire the shoes is a given; to do otherwise is to become a cultural refusenik, tantamount to class warfare.

The burden of class representation *requires* that we consume the things we are told to desire. *US Weekly,* for example, gives us specifics, listing products, prices, and details in Ingela Ratledge's article "The *Us* Buzz-o-Meter." The items for sale here include the Louis Vuitton satchel: "Louis Vuitton Satchel. Behold, the new gold standard: Jessica Simpson bagged this leather 'Le Fabuleux' tote ($2,720)" (34). We are urged to chill out like P. Diddy by choosing the same alcohol he drinks: "Effen Vodka. This super-smooth Dutch spirit—in regular and Black Cherry—boasts a rubber-wrapped bottle that keeps it chilled for P. Diddy, who likes it on the rocks. *Effen* cool! $30, liquor stores" (34). Supposedly we can even look like the Academy Award nominees Charlize Theron and Naomi Watts simply by purchasing the suggested makeup: "M.A.C. Oscar Palette. Nominees Charlize Theron and Naomi Watts each scored one of these custom-made kits, stocked with winning colors for eyes, cheeks and lips" (34).

All these invitations to class-pass as celebrities mask harsh social realities because, as Gordon Marshall notes in his study of class structure at the turn of the twentieth century, *Repositioning Class,* "it seems we may have mistaken changes in the *shape* of the class structure for changes in social fluidity. . . . More 'room at the top' has not been accompanied by greater equality in the opportunities to get there" (5). But reality be damned! As Deleuze and Guattari note, "man is the slave of the social machine" (254). We certainly have agency. We can shut off these images. We can be cultural refuseniks. But we suffer if we withdraw from society and its referents. We are absolutely kidding ourselves if we think we live in free bodies as free individuals in capitalist media culture. Our bodies are not ourselves. They are not ours. Neither are our desires.

In the Hollywood mythmaking machine, we sport what Pierre Bourdieu dubs the "body-for-others," and we are encouraged to equate mastery of the body with being rich. "One can never be too rich or too thin," goes the saying. The barrage of images endorsing this idea, indeed, *demanding* that we starve ourselves to perfection is almost impossible to avoid. In the past, fleshiness and fatness were associated with wealth. Now the thin body-for-others is absolutely tied to class status. Very few celebrities are allowed to be overweight. Few question the way the media portray Kate Winslet, for example, as overweight. Clearly, the media celebrate the massive weight loss of celebrities such as weatherman Al Roker and film critic Roger Ebert.

Filmmaker, actor, and director Vincent Gallo, apparently disgusted with Ebert's corpulent body, has feuded with Ebert, as depicted in *The Guardian Unlimited* and on VH1's *The 40 Greatest Celebrity Feuds*. Ebert allegedly made disparaging remarks about Gallo's film *Brown Bunny* (2003). Gallo, feeling rejected by the powerful critic, allegedly called Ebert "a fat pig with the physique of a slave trader," likening Ebert's appearance to that of a plantation owner (quoted in Peretti). Ebert's response was equally dismissive, admitting that although he was indeed fat, he could potentially diet and lose some weight, whereas Gallo would always be known as the director of *Brown Bunny*, which most critics agreed was a remarkably self-indulgent exercise in star-driven narcissism.

Perhaps we are moving toward a field of cultural images wherein "private persons are an illusion," for if celebrities have no privacy, why should anyone else (Deleuze and Guattari 264)? Hosts of programs offer us glimpses into the "private" worlds of celebrities. The fact is, however, nothing is private about the life of a celebrity.

The definition of celebrity demands constant images of the stars' private lives for our consumption. With the rise of "reality" television, we are now also barraged with images of real people as they class-pass into the public arena of celebrity where private persons indeed are an illusion. *Survivor, The Real World, Big Brother,* and many other reality shows *make* celebrities of people and reveal that celebrity is all about performing before the camera, giving up your privacy; eating snakes on *Fear Factor* or being punked on *Punk'd,* we are all celebrities—so says the television.

Indeed, we are not so much invited to class-pass as celebrities; we are demanded, commanded to do so. It is our manifest destiny, after all, implicit in the title of programs such as *Destination Stardom, 15 Seconds to Fame,* and *Pimp My Ride.* We can shop like the millionaire celebrity on Shop NBC, which offers a shopping program called *Beverly Hills Elegance.* Fuse offers a program from which we can learn to shop: *Celebrity Tastemaker.* The Do It Yourself (DIY) network has a program called *Celebrity Hobbies* in case we do not like golf, which we now learn how to fetishize by watching *Celebrity Golf* on, you guessed it, the Golf Channel.

Even pornography is classed and marked by class-passing. Playboy TV's *Celebrity Video Centerfold* offers us, on a typical program, *Jessica Hahn Unveiled.* Your every intimate desire is available via images from Time Warner Cable. The Fine Living Channel has a special on fulfilling your fantasy of owning "your private island." Jewelry is within your reach on Jewelry Television (ACN), which offers only two programs in rotation,

Gemstones and *Jewelry*. Listening to the celebrity host's soothing voice-over on gemstones, I quickly learn that the current offering of jewels is "bottled sunshine." The Arts and Entertainment Network (A&E), once a channel heavily programmed around the arts as well as celebrity, has moved into the desire and fantasy product with *House of Dreams*.

Similarly, the Learning Channel (TLC), which started out programming serious documentaries on everything from nature conservancy to world poverty, has moved over into celebrity mythmaking with several shows. On TLC's *Trading Spaces 100 Grand*, competitors receive fifty thousand dollars to spend on one room in a home, "making fantasies come true." Another TLC show is *World's Best Places to Strike It Rich;* one show concentrates on "extraordinary gambling destinations." If you are a serious gambler, you mustn't miss the Travel Channel's (Travel) episode of *World's Best,* which offers a rundown of the *Top Ten Vegas Casinos:* "Nearly 100 Las Vegas casinos bring in billions of dollars each year." Vegas, gambling, and showgirls are all rolled into one product placement ad on VH1's *Bootcamp: Showgirls,* in which five contestants (soon to be celebrities) compete for Las Vegas showgirl contracts.

Another offering in Fox's stable of television reality shows is *The Swan,* in which a group of supposedly unattractive young women are selected for extreme plastic surgery makeovers in the hopes that one of them will emerge so utterly transformed that she will be able to take her place on the catwalk as a celebrity fashion model. VH1's *All Access: Celebrity Sibling Showdown* offers the spectacle of sibling rivalry as a spectator sport, pitting media stars such as Serena and Venus Williams against each other in a mock contest to decide, among other things, which sister has the best "booty."

> Blood may be thicker than water, but it can't stop the divisive forces of VH1. Stay on your side of the room or we're gonna tell mom. *All Access: Celebrity Sibling Showdown* is going to settle the biggest sibling rivalries in pop culture—whether these kids like it or not. In this hour-long VH1 special, comedians, journalists and a family therapist will provide their wit, wisdom and totally irrelevant commentary on the biggest celebrity siblings. Paris vs. Nicky Hilton, Prince William vs. Prince Harry, Serena vs. Venus Williams, Barbara vs. Jenna Bush, Aaron vs. Nick Carter and many more will slug it out, round by round and blow by blow to determine who's the favorite . . . and who's not in categories like:

- who's hotter?
- who parties harder?
- who's got the better booty?
- who's more likely to be president?
- who's more likely to end up in a *Girls Gone Wild* video?
- who's got the better body?

and more! (*All Access* Web site)

The insatiable appetite for all things celebrity brings me to an interesting issue. The quest for fulfillment seems to be inherently unquenchable: it is the thirst that neither products nor association with celebrity can satisfy. This is a perfect quandary of capitalism because it means that if needs cannot be met, there will always be demand. This lack of fulfillment is what explains the frequent advertisements for antidepressants and antianxiety drugs, as well as those for myriad pharmaceuticals meant for stomach ailments, often shown during celebrity programming. The body-for-others can never be fulfilled, but you can ask your doctor about the little purple pill called Nexium for acid reflux, or you can calm your anxieties with an antidepressant.

One thing that seems unusual about wealth and consumption and the failure to be happy is, as Deleuze and Guattari note, a disappearance of pleasure and enjoyment: "In point of fact, something new occurs with the rise of the bourgeoisie: the disappearance of enjoyment as an end, the new conception of the conjunction according to which the sole end is abstract wealth and its realization in forms other than consumption" (254). If you are not enjoying something, if satisfaction is not the result of seeking pleasure in consumption, then perhaps a prescription for Strattera, for adult attention deficit disorder, may make things better or placate our desires.

Not only are we taught what products to desire and to embrace celebrity identity, but advertisers also suggest that perhaps that empty feeling we have may be filled by Prozac, Paxil, Zoloft, or any number of legalized drugs. Legalized sanctioned pursuit of pleasure and pampering is rampant in media imagery. Just so we know we are not alone in our pain, loneliness, and class anxiety, we can simply turn to Fit TV and check out some of the *World's Greatest Spas*. In Quebec you can visit the Thalassotherapy Center. An alternative is the Thai Body Glow Center.

You can always change your body with *Extreme Makeover*. Surgery to reduce fat or plump up the lips is encouraged; it is all a part of class-passing. After you *Shop Till You Drop* on the religious channel PAX, turn over to the Style Channel and check out the program called *Stripped: Read My Lips,* which tells the history of lip enhancement, including the use of collagen and silicone injections.

If you are impatient with the more traditional documentary style of *Stripped,* turn to VH1's *How Stars Get Hot 3,* and you can find out exactly how the celebrities use surgery, implants, and botox to achieve their celebrity look. If you can take it, turn on E!'s *Anna Bares All,* about Anna Nicole Smith's radical weight loss—"find out how she did it."

If you find yourself bored by the seemingly drugged-out voice of Anna Nicole Smith, simply turn to *Glamour* magazine, which offers a surefire method to "Find Your Ideal Weight." Alongside two photos of Renée Zellweger at different sizes (emaciated and voluptuous) is a small bulleted list of guideposts to "figure out your best look."

- Forget the scale. Instead, go to glamour.com to calculate your body mass index, which is better than a weight chart for measuring the healthiest weight for your height.
- Check out your family. Remember, being big in the hips or small in the bones runs in families. And yes, obesity may have a genetic link, but you can beat the odds by eating right and exercising as much as possible.
- Relearn the concepts of "full" and "hungry." Before meals, rate your hunger (1 being famished, 10 being stuffed). Eat slowly and ask yourself again. It's tough, but quitting at 5 rather than 10 is optimal, experts say. (141)

Again, fat is the mark of the lower classes, not tolerated by celebrity culture. A recent front-page pictorial article in the *National Enquirer,* about the shocking news that some celebrities have cellulite, has the ring of shock and moral outrage that should more properly be targeted at poverty, for example. We glimpse in "Celebrity Cellulite Exposed!" the alleged backsides of Jerry Hall, "supermodel" Stephanie Seymour, and Kristen Johnston (64–67). Their "crime" is equated with those of alleged murderers such as Robert Blake and O. J. Simpson. To be fat and a celebrity is to bring down civilization and the classes it houses in thin bodies.

A *People* magazine article gives away celebrity "Last Minute Diet Secrets" used to prepare for the Academy Awards ceremony. Vivica A. Fox admits, "I pop laxatives" (123). Tara Reid uses "starvation": "It makes a big difference. You look hot for a week, but you gain it all back" (123). Melissa Rivers tries to "work out like crazy" (123), and Sandra Bullock admits, "I sabotage myself. Before I put on an outfit, I just start to eat a lot. I don't know what's wrong with me" (122). Celebrities are painfully aware of the duty they have to remain thin to class-pass successfully. Even Oprah Winfrey, who spent years battling her weight, finally seems to be winning the battle. Along with her newly thin body, Oprah feels very comfortable with the trappings of celebrity from gowns to excessive weight loss regimens to daily brutal workouts.

In my opinion, Charlize Theron did not win an Academy Award for her performance in *Monster* (Patty Jenkins, 2003). She won the award for being able to gain weight and lose weight drastically and emphatically. Countless reports covered her "shocking" ability to lose the weight she gained to play a lower-class serial killer. The award was recognition not just for the weight gain and loss but also for Theron's class-passing, both on-screen and offscreen.

As a child, many articles noted, Charlize Theron came not from wealth and privilege but from a family in which she saw domestic abuse and murder firsthand. Her class-passing started with her modeling career and her near-anorexic figure. Furthermore, the Academy of Motion Picture Arts and Sciences rewarded her for being able to class-pass upward while experiencing the *déclassement* of excessive weight gain. But with her subsequent weight loss, she was met with the amazement we usually shower on religious mystics and saints who have witnessed acts of God. She is at once sacred and profane, class-passing simultaneously as the fat body of the actor and the fit body of the glamorous blonde celebrity. Winning the Academy Award for successfully class-passing is a thorny, politically charged act, but one would never think it for the lack of debate about it.

Oprah Winfrey took a break from her seemingly endless celebration of the 2003 Academy Awards, complete with a day-after program shot in the Kodak Theatre that featured an endless barrage of clips recapping the deadeningly boring event. A couple of days later, Oprah's program looked at the "shocking" news that young emphatically "middle-class" women, as young as fourteen, "from good homes . . . with loving parents," were increasingly turning to prostitution. On Oprah's set, tears were shed, stories were told, and Oprah repeatedly remarked that it was so "shocking" that these young girls came from better classes. We heard little discussion about *why* these young, fairly privileged girls go into prostitution. Each said simply, "It was just [for] the money." But no one stopped to ask why the young women felt they needed *so much* money. There were hints. Each girl told how her pimp took her shopping and how she was so excited to get away from home and to spend freely on luxury items, the items associated with celebrity.

These young women were simply trying to class-pass the best way they could. Society constantly tells them that they can and should have all the "bling" and the clothes of rap celebrities and actresses, such as Charlize Theron, Julia Roberts, and Oprah herself. Yet no one on the show even talked about why they felt their needs were not taken care of by the privileges of home and the middle class. They enact an example of bodies-for-others and class-passers. They are only working out the American Dream, which is all about consumption beyond one's means. Everybody seemed to miss this point, so "shocked" were they to find that women just like themselves and their children could and do go into prostitution.

What I found shocking, however, was that so little discussion concerned the young girls and boys from the lower classes who become prostitutes. An unspoken blame-the-victim mentality was palpable in the rhetoric of the show and its participants. Indeed, each time Oprah expressed her "shock" that middle-class teens could turn to prostitution, she implied that it is normal for poverty-stricken, poorly parented children who do not come from good homes to go into prostitution. Her implied classism was just as ugly as racism or sexism, but it went unnoticed. The audience endorsed the same unspoken dehumanization and denarration of the lower classes as well.

Shocking, also, was the lack of discussion about the middle-class and wealthy johns who comprise the clientele of these young, predominantly well-educated white, blonde middle-class hookers. A few of the former prostitutes themselves made disparaging remarks about the johns. They noted that they were doctors, lawyers, and professionals who often used the family SUV for a place to have sex with the prostitutes. Absolutely no discussion about the motivations of the "johns," or their desire to have sex with young, white, blonde, educated hookers who are just like their own daughters, was heard.

I came away from the show appalled and angry. Indeed, most of Winfrey's recent programs involve celebrity visits and strategic giveaways of products. The program about middle-class prostitution was a nod to the formerly socially aware Oprah, but now her seeming silence on the issue of class and privilege come from her comfort with privilege and her own class-passing.

On another eye-opening program a few weeks before the Academy Awards, Oprah met with a teary, overweight, and bloated Wynonna Judd, who wished to tell the public why she was having weight problems. She tried to explain the emptiness she felt inside, despite her success as a country-western singer. She explained that she came from poverty and felt as though she did not deserve her own success. This highlighted the hidden injuries of class-passing, an internalization of feeling unworthy. In response to her pain, she began eating and overeating.

An interesting exchange between Oprah and Wynonna then occurred. Oprah stopped Wynonna when she said she felt she did not deserve her success. Oprah disagreed and said she did not have that feeling. She said, "I'm a black girl from poverty. I don't have nothing [sic] to feel guilty about." Oprah's class-passing is related directly to her race. Upward mobility is expected, apparently, from those who are not white; thus race mobility is a form of class-passing. In this arena, at least, race trumps class.

One arena of performance that is centrally related to conspicuous consumption and class mobility is marriage, a multibillion-dollar industry supported by the celebrity industry with programs such as TLC's *A Perfect Wedding* and magazines such as *Modern Bride*. With regard to weddings, the sky is not the limit: there is no spending limit on extravagant weddings. Weddings themselves are performances of dreams; thus the phrase "the wedding of her dreams."

Young women of all classes, races, and sexualities are raised to think that the wedding itself is a transformative event. Beneath the messages, however, lurk the issues of class mobility and the performance of a spectacle of opulence and outrageous expense. Weddings are treated as though they are the single most important event in our lives. "It has to be perfect. . . . It's your wedding," reads an ad for formal wear from Men's Wearhouse (103). The high expectations for a wedding to be the "perfect" event practically ensures that it will never measure up to the fantasy.

Despite the current downturn in the economy, couples are denied no options in wedding spending. An advertisement from Scott Kay Platinum Jewelers in *Modern Bride* states, "Never compromise . . . when asking someone to spend the rest of their [sic] life with you" (2–3). A photograph of a couple is juxtaposed with the quote. We see a young woman and man in a black-and-white image. The charged look between the two says it all. Her face says, "There's no way you can afford this." His says, "I don't care. I'd give my life for you."

Clearly, economizing is not part of planning the class-passing event of your life. Your wedding is probably the only time that you will ever wear such expensive clothing. It is the one event in which you and your families must class-pass as upwardly mobile American success stories, but remember that it is a story, a narrative, with performers, actors, and directors. An article in *Modern Bride,* a magazine that supposedly caters to "every bride and every budget," instead gives only five price ranges for gowns: less than eight hundred dollars, less than fifteen hundred dollars, less than twenty-five hundred dollars, less than four thousand dollars, and more than four thousand dollars. In small type, we learn that "all engagement rings shown throughout start from $7,000" (Stylander 344).

In an advertisement for bridal jewels from a consortium of jewelers, readers are told to "indulge your fantasies with all that glitters" (Simon et al. 369). Another story encourages the bride into bankruptcy, touting the purchase of a designer wedding gown. "Runway Report" addresses the anxious and expectant consumer of bridal dreams. "There has never been a better time to be a bride. This season, designers continue to give you more choices, from slinky, sexy sheaths to big, bold gowns" (370). The final pages of the article feature outrageously expensive gowns for the mother of the bride. "After all, it's Mom's big day, too!" reads one caption (380). From the reception to the invitations, readers are encouraged to adopt the culture of classes above them and to perform as though they can afford to spend recklessly on wedding expenditures.

Indeed, the average cost of a wedding in the United States is about twenty-five thousand dollars, and 70 percent of engaged couples pay this expense themselves, thus starting out their married lives with massive debt (Putnam). But, as Carrie Ann Putnam notes, you can still have your dream wedding if you are willing to cut corners. Says Putnam,

> When my husband and I got engaged we knew we would pay for the wedding ourselves (125 guests), but we did not have $25,000 to spend! Nor did we want to put the bulk of our wedding on credit cards. But, with careful planning, we were able to have our dream wedding for approximately $12,000!" Yes, if you're willing to "lose the limos" ("You do not need limos to have a classy wedding!!!! . . . For example, my uncle has a gorgeous 700 series BMW, so I asked him to drive my parents and I to the Church. . . . For our attendants, I had two guests who both drive matching Ford Explorers drive the bridesmaids. . . .") and search through the clearance racks for the ultimate wedding gown ("I actually found my gown while leaning my weary body on a clearance rack! Although my dress had been used on a store model, there was absolutely nothing wrong with it. My dress was originally $1,200

and I stole it for $300!!!!!"), you, too, can get married in style for a mere $12,000 (Putnam).

TLC has a program that exploits young couples' obligation to pay for an expensive wedding. From another TLC program, *Perfect Proposal*, contestants are chosen to win a spot on the cruel and awkward *Perfect Wedding*. On *Perfect Wedding*, a couple wins an all-expenses-paid trip to an unknown destination from Orbitz. They are allowed to invite only fourteen guests. They are not told where they will be flying. They are told to pack one suitcase for a cold climate and one suitcase for a warm climate. In a rather cruel twist, the online viewers, rather than the bride and groom, get to choose all the accoutrements of the wedding, from the announcements to the color of the place settings. The contestants lose their composure when they discover they cannot invite more than fourteen people and find themselves disagreeing with the choices made by online viewers. When they start to cry because they are unable to invite treasured friends because of the fourteen-person limit, the producers surprise them by adding their friends to the list and having them surprise the bride and groom at the airport. It all seems cruel and exploitational and makes the viewer wonder why anyone would even want to get married on a reality television show. Looking at bridal-themed television shows and magazines, one is struck by the outright denial of the evidence of class and class struggle, but denial is perhaps a reflection of American amnesia and displacement of discussions about class. The importance placed on weddings strikes me as a form of terrorism procured through mass participation in events that demand silence around class. Consumer society performs a form of political terrorism that justifies second and third mortgages, debt, and, ultimately, bankruptcy and sadness.

Why, one wonders, do people put themselves through the tortures of commodified marriage? The debate about the rights of gays and lesbians to marry answers the question. Marriage itself is a structure of class mobility and economic privilege. The institution of marriage, which is an exclusionary practice, is a marker of class privilege. The treatment of gays and lesbians in our country has perhaps less to do with sexuality than it does with class, because gays and lesbians are treated as a lower class. In the same way that white people never seem to question, much less recognize, their own white privilege, many straight people never even recognize the privileges they are accorded in everyday life and, specifically, in marriage. Those who fight to "protect the sanctity of marriage" while trying to exclude gays and lesbians fail to recognize the rights for which lesbians and gays fight. An online article by Roedy Green outlines exactly what gays and lesbians deserve.

Gays call for the right to form legally recognized unions. Such unions would give gays the same rights that straights have, namely:

1. The right to choose your marriage partner.

2. The right to choose a marriage partner not a citizen of your country, and have it almost automatic [that] they be allowed to live in your country with you.

3. The right to visit your partner in hospital, even if the partner's blood family does not like you.

4. Income tax deductions for couples.

5. Pension benefits and other spousal benefits such as company medical and dental plans.

6. Wherever the term *"spouse"* appears in law, it also apply to gay couples who have formed a legally recognized union.

7. The right to custody of children by a previous heterosexual marriage.

8. The right to adopt children.

9. The right to claim their partner or their partner's children as dependents on income-tax forms.

10. The right to transfer registered retirement savings plans to surviving homosexual partners without paying taxes the way straight couples can.

11. Same-sex couples should not be forced to testify against each other, just as heterosexual couples are protected.

12. That this same-sex union be called marriage. If it had some other name, the union would have the separate-but-equal problem that plagues segregation. It would inevitably be different from heterosexual marriage with second-class status. Only by calling it marriage do all the benefits and responsibilities mentioned in hundreds of acts of parliament automatically come into effect. This is the quickest route to full equality.

Gays and lesbians have long enjoyed the right to marry in the Netherlands and other enlightened nations in which homosexuality is not used as a form of *déclassement*. Straight or gay, we are all alike in our humanistic wants and needs; why are we so slow to recognize this simple fact?

In the past few years, Bravo has been running the program *Gay Weddings* and even the *New York Times* is now publishing same-sex wedding announcements. Those who fight against the rights of same-sex couples sense that their entitlement as a privileged class is crumbling. It is only a matter of time and justice before this new civil rights issue will finally see justice. Perhaps the time has come that all subalterns, whether declassed because of sexuality, gender, ethnicity, or other identity markers, begin to see that the fundamental issue is class. When the rights of gays and lesbians are finally recognized in this country, this group will no longer be reduced to second-class citizenship. The upside is the rights they will gain in terms of legality, human rights, marriage protections, tax deductions, and so forth. The only possible downside is that gays and lesbians will then be full participants in the conspicuous consumption associated with marriage. This is a factor that marriage industry professionals, who will make even more profits with the emancipation of gay and lesbian peoples, no doubt recognize. As for the arguments that gay and lesbian marriages will "rock civilization as we know it," one has only to reply that gays and lesbians have been living together for thousands of years. If anything, the right to marry is actually a rather conservative agenda, which would work toward true "family values," in which all people, despite their sexuality, are allowed to fulfill their role in the American family.

5
Live in Your World, Class-Pass in Ours

The defining terms we have traditionally used to discuss *class* and *class mobility* are outdated and outmoded. Terms such as *blue-collar* and *white-collar* are as dated as the concepts of neat, distinctive categories such as "high culture," "middle culture," and "low culture." Fantasies of cultural mobility are so pernicious throughout popular culture that the realities of classed experience are frequently masked and perhaps even, arguably, surpassed in importance by postmodern ideas about the self and performed identity.

Throughout popular culture we find rampant evidence of mass media's consumption and replication of the performing postmodern body, or what Steven Shaviro dubs "the hollowness of the performing self" (115). Nowhere is this more evident than in the disconnect between class fantasy (unconsciousness) and economic and cultural realities that are repressed and ignored, such as voter disenfranchisement and the demonization of academe.

We are steeped in images and fantasies of class-passing, especially those fantasies that portray a society in which the only class stature we are encouraged to aspire to is that of the celebrity. Thus MTV offers the program *I Want a Famous Face*, in which viewers can engage in participatory fantasies of people who not only aspire to celebrity class but also are willing to undergo plastic surgery or whatever else is necessary to become or class-pass as, for example, Britney Spears. The Web site for *I Want a Famous Face* rhetorically asks, "How far would you go to look like a celebrity? Nose job here? Nip and tuck there? The people [on this series] went that far and beyond. They have endured painful and sometimes risky reconstructive surgery to look like their favorite celebrity."

Mia, one young woman on the series, believed that by undergoing such a radical transformation, she would jump-start her career as an entertainer. As MTV summarized her quest, "Mia believes she already naturally looks like Britney, she just needs the breasts. She hopes that with her breast implants, she will be able to quit her day job and make it big-time as an entertainer" (*I Want a Famous Face—Meet the Patients* Web site).

In an interview after the surgery, Mia reflected on the transformational process.

> *MTV:* Are you pleased with the results of your surgery?
> *Mia:* Yes! Very much so!
> *MTV:* Was it worth it? Why or why not?
> *Mia:* Yes—it was worth it because I really wanted to do it for me.
> *MTV:* What was the biggest post-surgery surprise?
> *Mia:* How much pain I was in and also how out of it I was.
> *MTV:* Since the surgery, have you been mistaken for Britney?
> *Mia:* No more than I was before the surgery. (*I Want a Famous Face—Meet the Patients* Web site)

In view of this outcome, one has to ask, "Was this makeover *really* necessary?" But apparently Mia is satisfied, and her dreams of fantasy stardom are on the verge of being fulfilled. The chance to remake ourselves in the image of the famous is all that we ask.

The show is a metanarrative for the millions of people who fantasize about becoming Britney Spears, with an actual and disturbingly real example of a young woman who is completely deluded and fancies herself a Britney Spears look-alike. She undergoes painful plastic surgery for breast implants on camera to pursue her dream to become Britney Spears. She's clearly driven by personal fantasies, but she enacts a mass cultural phenomenon that should not go unnoticed.

Class consciousness becomes unconsciousness in celebrity popular culture that unconsciously mounts an attack on intellect, truth, and facts, facts such as those laid bare in Michael Shnayerson's *Vanity Fair* exposé, "Hack the Vote." Shnayerson's piece demonstrates that the 2000 presidential election debacle in Florida was only a harbinger of things to come if something is not done about the glitch-prone and easily hacked electronic voting machines now being installed in all fifty states.

This story really should be the number one story in all media outlets, in print, video, and on the Internet, but instead we are offered increasingly more celebrity fantasy, such as the photo spread of the glamorous gowns actresses wore to the Screen Actors Guild Awards in the *People* magazine article "Class Act." Jennifer Garner naturalizes class-passing with her statement, "Ralph Lauren was an easy choice. I always feel so great wearing his clothes" (Lynch et al. 46).

Actresses shift change in "Class Act," and readers are encouraged to coperform celebrity class-passing ("Jennifer Garner in a $69,000 Van Cleef & Arpels ruby brooch" [Lynch et al. 48]), while most of society is quietly being stripped of one of the most basic rights of Americans, the right to vote. Shnayerson points out that the touch-screen voting machines, the majority of which four companies manufacture, "three of which have ties to wealthy Republicans," will have their machines in almost every state in the union, counting votes in the presidential election (158).

Far from being a conspiracy theorist piece, the *Vanity Fair* article carefully explains how the new machines are almost guaranteed to yield manipulated results, honestly inaccurate results, or both. Among the astounding revelations, "a fifty-two-year-old freelance writer, literary publicist, and grandmother from Seattle named Bev Harris" uncovered is that the new systems have the capability to record *negative votes* (Shnayerson 160). In other words, a hacker or voting supervisor can easily remove votes. "Why," Harris wondered, "would there *ever* be cause to record negative votes in an electronic voting machine" (162)?

Furthermore, Shnayerson reported, Harris was easily able to download information and voting supervisor passwords from a Web site she found with a simple Google search on the Internet. Harris managed to hack into an AccuVote central server easily and found out just how incredibly easy manipulating vote totals is. She tried out her theory.

> On the AccuVote central server, Harris believed, a supervisor would see votes coming in on his screen through a program called GEMS. But behind it, like a second set of books, was the database engine usable by Microsoft Access, where the vote totals were stored. With a couple of mouse clicks, Harris was able to go in through Microsoft Access, as if through a back door, change vote totals, and erase any "audit trail" of her actions. The supervisor looking at his screen on GEMS would see the new tally and have no idea it had been doctored by a hacker. (Shnayerson 162)

Harris and others learned that furthermore, the companies who manufacture the voting machines, such as Diebold, appeared to be well aware of the system's inadequacies, but they nevertheless sold and installed them. The failure rate of the voting machines, above and beyond their insecurity, is well known in the industry. One installer, a subcontractor named Rob Behlor, is quoted as saying, "Don't expect a lot—they're broke, man. They do crazy crap, and they don't do the same crazy crap twice," adding, "And here's the really scary thing: you could test the machine and it would test fine, then you'd turn it off, power it up again, and it would fail" (Shnayerson 167, 168).

The lengthy *Vanity Fair* article recounts the discrepancies, failure rate, and details about the alarming insecurity of the voting machines. Harris has also authored a book, *Black Box Voting: Ballot Tampering in the 21st Century,* which describes the system's inadequacies. Nevertheless, the supposedly liberal media have expressed minimal interest in the voting-machine scandal. Other than a few stories in *Atlantic Monthly, Newsweek,* and the *New Yorker,* the story concerning the voting machines received scant coverage by the media, yet that same media have seemingly endless pages to devote to the lives of Jessica Simpson, Hilary Duff, Britney Spears, and Justin Timberlake. Stories concerning possible voter fraud and ballot tampering have been almost erased since the 2004 election. Still many are concerned about problems and irregularities during that election, in Ohio for example. But these stories are dismissed as sour grapes. Besides voter disenfranchisement will never be as sexy as the latest celebrity gossip.

Class struggle is no longer about labor unions, corporate takeovers, and the loss of jobs to free trade. Class struggle is deeply embroiled in the pages of celebrity fantasy that declass us all into positions of submission and utterly deluded fantasies such as boob-jobbing our way into the life of Britney Spears. Even celebrity artist Quddus complains in an issue of *YM* that we are wasting too much time on celebrity: "I don't like how overexposed the personal lives of celebrities are. I haven't been able to look at a magazine without feeling like I'm stalking Britney. I mean, is it just me, or doesn't maintaining your own love life take up enough of your attention?" (80).

This article appears, ironically, in an issue of *YM* almost exclusively dedicated to insisting that class mobility is deeply connected to passing as a celebrity, identifying with a celebrity, and celebrity profiles. The April 2004 *YM* issue gives one a sense of how celebrity discourse shapes class mobility. Old Navy, in collaboration with Fox's *American Idol,* asks the reader, "Want to get the star treatment?" in an ad that cross-promotes *American Idol* and Old Navy brand: "You could be a VIP. . . . Get EXCLU-SIVE ACCESS to an *Idol*'s pre-show rehearsal. . . . Be red-carpet ready. . . . Just bring this card to an Old Navy store. . . . Take off to L.A. with three friends and see an *American Idol* show *live*" (47). In case one has not had enough faux celebrity-passing and fantasies of becoming an American idol, another ad follows, this one for the *American Idol* Collectible Card Game. "Watched the show. . . . Heard the song. . . . Listened to the judges. . . . But missed the audition. . . . Even if you can't sing, YOU CAN PLAY *American Idol* Collectible Card Game!" (Fremantle 129). Over and over, the message is that you, too, can be a star.

YM is a mass-marketed magazine targeted to young women. These young women, who might be encouraged more profitably to read about their future voter disenfranchisement and the resultant class immobility, instead are offered an inane and bizarre display of fetishized products and people who are used to promise class mobility while they practically en-sure déclassement and the ignorance that goes with déclassement. In a section on the beauty secrets of the stars, for example, readers can fanta-size about "Star Treatments" while their voting rights and civil rights are being systematically destroyed.

> Whenever you see your favorite singer or actress looking gorgeous and flawlessly made up on the red carpet, chances are there's a troop of hair, makeup, and nail pros behind the scenes to thank for it. Now that a few of our favorite celebrity stylists have their very own product lines, we common folk can enjoy some of the same Hollywood beautifying benefits. So what if we have to apply the stuff ourselves? (Fedida 34)

Certainly, *YM* is not completely ignorant of young women's desires for class mobility. Indeed, many articles concern and address class mobility, but from a celebrity-obsessed viewpoint. For example, *YM* offers examples of role models to emulate in a page called "Fame Game." Here we learn how "Vanessa Minnillo went from Miss Teen U.S.A. to [MTV's] *TRL* [*Total Request Live*] host. See, good *can* come from beauty pageants" (Onion 82). "Career CPR" opines, "To get your career off the ground or jump-start a flailing one, land a show on MTV. Hey it worked for Ashton Kutcher" (82). Class mobility is rarely, if ever, linked to education, the traditional mode of class rise; instead, it is associated with brands such as Maybelline and Target.

Class is at the center of self-actualization in comparing actress Lind-say Lohan with celebrity Nicole Richie, in Beth Shapouri's essay "Class vs. Crass." The two celebrities are compared according to class lines, but the criteria for estimating class are sporting a trendy hairstyle and using the correct beauty products rather than making informed college or ca-reer choices. Next to the photo of Lindsay Lohan, the star of the comedy *Confessions of a Teenage Drama Queen,* who portrays "class" over "crass," we read this entry:

> It's kind of hard to put a finger on what exactly makes us love Lindsay Lohan's style so much. Maybe it's how shiny her long red hair is. Or that her berry lip-gloss and blush are in the same color family, so they complement each other perfectly. We're also partial to her thick, mas-cara-clump-free lashes. Very nice indeed. (32)

Conversely, of Nicole Richie, who here is associated with downward mobility, tackiness, and "crass," we read,

> No one ever accused Nicole Richie of looking elegant. And this picture demonstrates why. That mop of stringy, multicolored hair is kind of terrifying. And we could definitely do without the over-the-top überfake lashes. As for that super-frosted hot-pink lipstick, that reeks of 1984 . . . enough said. (32)

Clearly, the *YM* editors are aware that their young readers are inter-ested in the hows and means of class rise, especially evidenced in the ar-ticle "A Girl's Guide to Becoming a Lady." Here, class is displayed as the "other white marker," so to speak. Class is ineluctably linked to white-ness, so much so that the ethereal and pasty white figures literally wash off the pages. They are whiter than the background. This article is a true throwback to an earlier time, with lines such as "a true lady must never forget her classic red lipstick" (106), "avoid fussing with your hair, clothes, makeup, and dare we say it, shoes during meals" (106), and "you can never go wrong with classic pearls" (108).

Again, class mobility is associated with products and performance and is inextricably linked to celebrity and designers such as Ralph Lauren and Steve Madden. This article is intriguing because its phrases are reminis-cent of those of Emily Post, demonstrating that old-fashioned notions about class mobility, shorn of their messages about the importance of a good education, can be injected into a message of the plausibility of ce-lebrity class-passing.

These messages are clearly informed by outmoded ideas about class and are reinforced in the Maybelline ad, which is in itself a great example of a hybrid mixture of old class mobility meets new class mobility. In the ad, celebrity Josie Moran is shown wearing "wet shine diamonds, rhinestone pink" lipstick and nail polish. The color and metallic finish are clearly hyperreal—no such color exists in nature—yet Maybelline uses its signature catchphrase, which itself hints of the old aristocratic class system, in which class is a hereditary trait: "Maybe she's born with it. Maybe it's Maybelline." Of course, it's Maybelline.

No one is born with hot pink metallic lips and nails. The disconnect here is almost as jarring as the vision of the young woman who deludes herself into thinking that her massive fake breasts make her look anything like Britney Spears in *I Want a Famous Face*. Offered here are delusions mixed with fantasy; no room for the harsh realities of election fraud, economic realities, or the need for a good education. Looking at the ads in the back of *YM* I found a few references to education, including ads for John Casablanca's modeling school, Barbizon Modeling School, high school diploma "thru [sic] home study," and art instruction school.

As if to put a nail in the coffin, the back page insert article in *YM* is an outright critique of the value of high school itself. "What I Was Like in High School" covers the high school years of MTV's *TRL* celebrity VJ Damien Fahey. "In high school, I could've given two craps about math. Now I count down from 10 to one everyday," brags Fahey (154). Fahey's recounting of his high school days supports the notion that school is worthless except for the opportunities it provides for prankster behavior.

> I was really shy during my first two years at Longmeadow High School in Massachusetts because I didn't know a lot of people. I moved to Longmeadow in sixth grade, and most of the kids from my middle school went to a different high school. I had a couple of friends who I hung out with, but my main focus was working at the local radio station, WMAS, a small adult-contemporary channel. Eventually, I got a job as a weekend DJ.
>
> By junior year a buzz went around school that I was on the radio, and all of a sudden I started having more friends. During junior and senior years, I was probably the most outgoing kid in class and was always making jokes. One time I got those capsules that smell like eggs, and a friend and I dropped two or three in the hallway. They had to evacuate one side of the school! They never found out it was us, though.

Then at the senior prom, in 1999, someone (not me) pushed a giant potted plant off a balcony—we were up, like, five stories—and it broke a lady's car windshield. Somehow my name got thrown into the mix of who did it, and because I was known for being a silly prankster, I took the brunt of the blame and got a couple of detentions. It sucked. (154)

America is suspended in a sad state of class unconsciousness. Indeed, most Americans have convinced themselves that class-consciousness is not a problem in the United States. In his brilliant analytical article in *Harper's,* "Lie Down for America: How the Republican Party Sows Ruin on the Great Plains," Thomas Frank notes that the United States is split into the red states and the blue states, at least rhetorically, and that this split is not just related to those for whom the red states and blue states voted in the 2000 election but also very much related to class. The red-stater is portrayed, Frank argues, as a "regular down-home working stiff" (39).

One of the mantras of what Frank dubs "the two Americas literatures" is that "class doesn't matter to the noble proletarians of Bush country" (39). Red-staters, as the myth goes, "have no class resentment or class consciousness" (39). They vote against their own interests. Why working-class people vote against their own interests is the main question that Frank seeks to answer. Red-state working people vote for Republicans who consistently vote to make things better for the very rich and worse for the middle and lower classes.

The right has managed to convince the once liberal, even radical, Kansas voters, for example, to abandon their class-consciousness and vote in the interest of millionaires. Frank notes that deregulated capitalism has given Kansas and all Midwesterners a collapsed farm economy. Wal-Marts put smaller merchants out of business as huge agribusiness conglomerates put family farms out of business. Free-market policies moved jobs out of the United States, and Kansas, like many midwestern states, is a shadow of its former self.

Why on earth would Kansans and Nebraskans, for example, vote against their interests? The reasons are quite complex, but they certainly return to the question of education and the influences of mass media. Frank declares,

Not too long ago, Kansans would have responded to the current situation by making the bastards pay. This would have been a political certainty, as predictable as what happens when you touch a match to a puddle of gasoline. When business screwed the farmers and the workers—when it implemented monopoly strategies invasive beyond the

Populists' worst imaginings, when it ripped off shareholders and casu-
ally tossed thousands out of work—you could be damned sure about
what would follow. . . . Not these days. Out here the gravity of discon-
tent pulls in only one direction: to the right, to the right, further to the
right. Strip today's Kansans of their job security and they head out to
become registered Republicans. Push them off their land and the next
thing you know they're protesting in front of abortion clinics. Squander their life savings on manicures for the CEO and there's a good
chance they'll join the John Birch Society. But ask them about the rem-
edies their ancestors proposed—unions, antitrust laws, public ownership—and you might as well be referring to the days when knighthood
was in flower. . . . Let us pause for a moment and gaze across this landscape of dysfunction. A state is spectacularly ill served by the Reagan-
Bush stampede of deregulation, privatization, and laissez-faire. It sees
its countryside depopulated, its towns disintegrate, its cities stagnate—
and its wealthy enclaves sparkle, behind their remote-controlled security gates. The state erupts in revolt, making headlines around the world
with its bold defiance of convention. But what do its revolutionaries
demand? More of the very measures that have brought ruination on
them and their neighbors in the first place. This is not just the mystery
of Kansas; this is the mystery of America, the historical shift that has
made it all possible. (46)

One could even argue that voting against your own class is a variant
on downward class-passing, a twisted form of identifying with one's own
oppressor. The class unconsciousness of *YM*, then, is really not that far
from the class unconsciousness going on in the minds of the red-state
voters. In both *YM* and popular culture, class-consciousness is associated
with Marxism, liberalism, and the elite, especially academe. Academe is
associated in pop culture with all things "immoral," whether it be the
funding for art from the National Endowment for the Arts or the study
of snobbish and elite subjects such as literature and art. When academic
professionals are portrayed in films, they are often sexual predators, evil
monsters, or people completely out of touch with the world. This sinis-
ter approach to academe and teachers is exemplified in scores of films and
is an attack on the classedness of the educated elite.

Wonder Boys (Scott Rudin, 2000) stars Michael Douglas as a fairly
lecherous, pot-smoking, adulterous professor and writer who works on
a worthless second novel and engages in a tawdry affair with his colleague,
played by Frances McDormand. Although he is washed up as a writer,

he manages to hold down a job at an elite school despite his questionable behavior and mediocrity. In the teen-oriented horror film *The Faculty* (Robert Rodriguez, 1998), the Herrington High School faculty comprises monsters from outer space, including actors Salma Hayek, Bebe Neuwirth, Robert Patrick, Piper Laurie, Famke Janssen, and Daniel von Bargen. Their monstrous behavior not only adheres to the norms of popular culture narrative, but it is also a commentary on the way students actually do feel oppressed by their teachers. Gus van Sant's *Elephant* (2003), a fictionalized treatment of the real-life tragedy at Columbine High School, where students massacred their peers, puts some of the blame on the cluelessness of the teachers who, because of their upper-classedness and bookishness, ignored the needs of the misunderstood killers.

Todd Solondz's brilliant *Welcome to the Dollhouse* (1995) concentrates on the plight of misfit middle-class Dawn Wiener (Heather Matarazzo), whose teachers treat her with utter indifference even as she is subjected to degrading abuse by other high school students. *Rock 'n Roll High School* (Allan Arkush, 1979) includes an over-the-top performance by Mary Woronov as a sadistic high school principal. Michael Caine was nominated for an Academy Award for his performance as the alcoholic professor Frank Bryant in *Educating Rita* (Lewis Gilbert, 1983). Class difference is at the center of this film. Julie Walters was also nominated for an Academy Award for her performance as Rita, a cockney working-class hairdresser who signs up for adult education classes. She chooses Bryant as a tutor but finds he is much more interested in drinking than in thinking.

Educating Rita is less a critique of academe, however, than a critique of the British class system. Nevertheless, the film is important for its depiction of yet another alcoholic professor who becomes involved with his students. Rita sees through his pretentiousness and is painted as the better person of the two, but then again working-class people are almost always better morally than academics in British pop culture.

Harold Pinter penned the quintessential study of effete, immoral, and weak academic men in *Accident* (Joseph Losey, 1967). Dirk Bogarde plays an Oxford University don who wastes no time becoming deeply involved in relationships with seemingly lost and innocent graduate students Michael York and Jacqueline Sassard. Stanley Baker, an even more lecherous professor, has an affair with Sassard. Losey's work admirably captures the repressed sexuality in academe, especially at Oxford against the backdrop of the 1960s and the loosening of sexual mores.

Another 1960s critique of the morality of academics is *Who's Afraid of Virginia Woolf?* (Mike Nichols, 1966). Elizabeth Taylor and Richard Burton star in this incisive exploration of the lives of decadent and amoral professors. Many of the films discussed here are great films, and I mention them to familiarize the reader with some stock characters in popular culture that are representative of academe.

Contempt for academe is a common theme in many facets of popular culture. Higher education is no longer necessary, at least according to many television programs that favor bling over brains. Anna Nicole Smith can barely put together a sentence, yet she is celebrated for bagging a wealthy millionaire and flaunting her ignorance. Another example of movement away from the support of higher education is seen in satirical work. In such a satire, *Instant Status: Or How to become a Pillar of the Upper Middle Class,* Charles Merrell Smith sets a smart-aleck tone and quips that whereas "the alert aspirant for a place in the corporate sun will see immediately that while a college degree is almost mandatory equipment, there is no need for him to obtain an education" (65). Academe is a class-passing machine, after all. Paul Fussell notes, "Some of the most assiduous social climbers are university professors" (170). The problem with class-passing through academe, however, is that it often results in alienation and vulnerability. As Sennett and Cobb note in their study *The Hidden Injuries of Class,*

> those who change class, through a white-collar job or a higher level of education, feel terribly ambivalent about their success and the ambivalence they treat as a sign of vulnerability in themselves. Those who make reasonably comfortable lives for themselves and their families as workers, who cope without leaving the arena of manual labor, are also touched by the feeling of a powerlessness embedded in the self. (36–37)

Performing the self as an academic who is a class-passer is often a painful experience. Class makes people performers and spectators. Academics are suspect not only in their own eyes but also in the eyes of people from all classes outside academe. Many have suggested that academe is itself a class outside the traditional class distinctions. This concept is interesting because class is therefore not always seen as a liberator or indeed positive quality worth attaining. Class can be a limitation. It can ostracize you from other people. Class constricts and limits relationships.

Class-passing in academe causes "status incongruity" or a feeling of being caught between two worlds (Sennet and Cobb 21). A collective of situationists notes that the students themselves are subject to a form of status incongruity.

> The student is a stoical slave: the more chains authority binds him with, the freer he thinks he is. Like his new family, the university, he takes himself for the most "independent" social being, whereas he is in fact *directly and conjointly* subservient to the two most powerful systems of social authority: the family and the state. He is their well-behaved and grateful child. Following the logic of the *submissive child,* he shares all the values and mystifications of the system and concentrates them in himself. The illusions that formerly had to be imposed on white-col-lar workers are now willingly internalized and transmitted by the mass of future lower cadres. (321)

In a similar vein, Stanley Aronowitz notes that both Pierre Bordieu and Louis Althusser see school as an "ideological state apparatus" (Aronowitz, *Politics* 50). In this world, students must class-pass as a means of social survival, as new, competing cliques are born and as the rapid pace of contemporary social discourse subsequently extinguishes them. In such a situation, all that one can dream of is the possibility of escape—free-dom from the arbitrary rules that bind the students to the institutions they are forced to inhabit. Because genuine mobility is an impossibility for most students, only one avenue of self-expression remains for the millennial student: the world of cyberspace. Able to transform himself or herself into myriad competing identities for various role-playing games, able to class-pass in a world in which the very concept of identity is constantly mu-table, twenty-first-century adolescents find phantasmal release from the exigencies of their existence in games such as *Samurai Warriors, Narc, Plague of Darkness, Fable, Half-Life 2,* and a host of other alternative cyber universes.

Sony's PlayStation 2 is the most popular video game platform; Xbox ranks a distant second. The average video game costs fifty dollars when it first appears on the market; some are thirty or forty dollars, but fifty is the average price. That's why rentals are such a big business, and there's also the repetition factor: once you play a game a few dozen times, you get to know the strategy of the game so well that it becomes boring. Because of this, few players own their own games, preferring to rent the newest and hottest titles. In addition, most of the newer games are Internet-capable, which means that each player can go online and play with other gamers. Thus he or she can adopt an identity for the game that has little to do with his or her real persona. This "cyberpassing" has given rise to the increasingly pervasive practice of class-passing in cyberspace. The concept of virtual class-passing would seem inherently Foucaultian by some, but for digital theorist Henry Jenkins, "cyberspace provides a place to experiment with alternative structures of government, new forms of social relations, which may, at least on the most grassroots of levels, allow us to temporarily escape, if not fully transform, unacceptable social conditions in our everyday lives" (243).

Indeed, cyberpassing allows and invites players to build both classless worlds and to play with the classed worlds they experience in real life. Opportunities abound for class, race, gender, and corporeal passing, not to mention class mimicry and class minstrelsy. Players experientially embrace utopian notions about class and larger notions about leaving the classed, raced, and gendered order of the real. Cyberspace and digital technology offer "a toolkit for social and political transformation" (Jenkins 242). One need only "live" in the real world to be able, as PlayStation's slogan goes, to play in theirs.

The advertisements for digital video games stress, unsurprisingly, that the players are in command. Although film ads stress the things to which you will be subjected (visions of destruction, romance, hot actors, mind-bending narratives, and so forth), video game ads stress the first-person imperative actions and twists that the player can do. Many advertisements almost sound like orders from the distributors and makers of video games. For example, PlayStation's ad for a game called *Fight Night 2004* directly addresses the player with comments such as "Bob and weave to wear 'em down. Or bait opponents with fakes to set 'em up for the canvas nap," and "Create openings and close 'em hard with brutal accuracy and timing" (6–7). Repeatedly, the emphasis is on the control the interactive player has over the virtual world. Similarly, an advertisement for Xbox's *Breakdown* implores the player to "fight a legion of super-human soldiers," and "unlock new punching and kicking combinations" (10). *Breakdown* even promises to aid you in leaving reality and entering your subconscious.

The oft-repeated slogan for *Breakdown* is, "The subconscious is a state in which reality is just a visitor" (10–11). Nevertheless, reality and its subconscious have a way of entering the cyberworld. Obviously, this militarist game's invention is spawned by the collective unconscious of a country at war, as are so many other video games that draw on imagery, plot, and the "blood and gore" and "intensive violence" (11) that subconsciously refer to the real wars we are engaged in as a state. Real wars, which players have little or no authority over, disempower the men and women who play these games. In the real world, they can be sent off to war to experience a real-life version of *Breakdown*'s cyberworld, which promises a "compelling military/science fiction storyline [that] will turn players' [minds] upside down" (10). *Breakdown* plays on real-life fears, anxieties, and thrill seeking, as well as adrenaline-pumping nonfiction, to sell "a revolutionary combination of hand-to-hand combat and weapons-based fighting" (10).

Video games dredge the conscious and subconscious for their themes, and the call to war is prominent among a current crop of games, such as Tom Clancy's *Splinter Cell, Rainbow Six 3,* and *Ghost Recon: Jungle Storm.* The lavish ad for these three games (70–82) quotes a fictitious U.S. Navy Seal operative next to an aestheticized photo of a section of a male torso, which shows a uniformed male hand on a machine gun (74–75). The unnamed Navy Seal notes, "It is often the little things that will kill you" (75). While offering escape from reality and control in cyberspace, the language of the advertisement for *Vigilance* lets the reader know quite clearly that this Tom Clancy–based game is as close to "real" as possible.

> Even the best-laid plans don't withstand the first five minutes of combat. To succeed, each team member must be watchful of subtle, unpredictable nuances in ballistics, enemy behavior, and the environment. To reproduce the minute details of real-life operations, the Clancy Games Development Team looks beyond second accounts, drawing upon their own military experiences as former U.S. Marines, National Guard Reserve servicemen, and Military Police. Some details are too critical to be handled without the deadliest of certainty. (75)

"There's just something about leveling a village that's really, really satisfying" is a frightening caption found alongside a shot of a militaristic shot from *Goblin Commander* (Bryant 50). According to the reviewer, Patrick Bryant, *Goblin Commander* "puts you in control of a goblin clan as they chop their way through armies of other goblins" (50). The player is emphatically in control as he or she certainly might not be in true mortal combat. *Goblin Commander* offers a space in which "combat is swift and smooth; the level of control you receive over your goblin's rampage works well" (50).

In repeatedly emphasizing the control and power the player has over war games such as *Full Spectrum Warrior,* the advertisements for these games inevitably remind us of the subconscious and conscious fears we have about loss of control and power and other obstacles experienced in real combat. What is denarrated then—lack of control, lack of power, lack of leadership, chaos, pain, death, and all the psychological harms of war—actually sell the product. The denarrated real buttresses the unreal. The review for *Full Spectrum Warrior* in *Xbox Nation,* the magazine for Xbox owners, opens with an ode to individualism and total control: "Be an army of one with your Xbox controller" (56). Still in development, *Full Spectrum Warrior* is a "real-time, squad-based army simulator," and the lack of control over others is built into the game that the player controls in a bit of irony (56). Thus the mixture of control and lack of control is another selling point.

> We recently enlisted in *Warrior*'s fictitious wartime scenario with a lengthy hands-on test and came away shell shocked and slack. Despite the game's innovative approach it's a strategy game viewed from the middle of the action—you issue orders to your team, but never directly control the movement or aim of a single character. (56)

Documentary-like details that hint at reality sell *Full Spectrum Warrior.* For those who seek an even closer approximation of war, Pandemic, the developer of the game, offers the opportunity to play the original version, which was designed for U.S. Army training purposes: "Like a real squad leader, you'll need to heed audio cues from your men for pertinent game information. Those who finish authentic mode have the option of uploading their best times online. Masochism is alive and well on Xbox" (56).

Masochism may be alive and well on Xbox, as it is in the real world, but that is an interesting selling point for a game that promises control. But as the advertisement for the three Tom Clancy video games notes, "freedom isn't free" and wars must be fought that involve both sadism and masochism (*Splinter Cell* 80). If "the whole point of being an American is to enjoy your freedom," then being an American involves an endless return to warfare and combat because "when the threat is extinguished, and the cost of freedom is clear—they will readily fight again. *When your moment comes, how will you perform?*" (81).

The copy in this twelve-page ad is nothing short of agit-prop for continual war. The ad is a fantastic recruitment tool as well as an interesting call to players to pass into the class of war hero. To market the games as close to reality, "the Clancy Games Development Team volunteered for unprotected tear gas exposure and trained with non-lethal munitions used by militaries to condition troops to fear. These experiences aided teams in depicting the crucial seconds of combat tension" (75).

Another video game specifically notes that it is based on real class conditions of the men who die by the millions in "history's meat grinder" ("New School" 102). *Call of Duty: Finest Hour* reminds me of politicians who use their war experiences to validate themselves, not just as heroes but as distinctly classed heroes, or grunts.

> No matter how many times you've single-handedly stopped the Wehrmacht on your TV screen, supersoldiers don't win world wars in real life—heroes emerge only after nations throw grunts by the million into history's meat grinder. *Call of Duty: Finest Hour* "emphasizes 'everyman' characters who heed their own call of duty for a great variety of reasons," says Producer Scott Langteau, top brass behind the historical shooter. ("New School" 102)

Although *Call of Duty: Finest Hour* promises the experiential class-based drama of the grunt, the everyman, and the real-life war heroes of the past, it also offers the opportunity to class-pass and gender-pass as a female sniper or a Russian tanker. Depending on the player you draw, you play the game either taking or receiving orders.

> You'll assume the roles of characters who range from a Russian tanker charged with defending a besieged Stalingrad, to a female sniper liberating her hometown, to an American GI escorting a 155 mm howitzer into the heart of Aachen, to name a few. As that Soviet conscript, you won't simply sit astride 33 tons of screeching steel. (What's warfare without hardware?) Instead, you'll take control of the tank and run the goose-steppers into the ground. Dozens of friendly soldiers will fight alongside you and, depending on your rank, lead the charge or accept orders. ("New School" 102)

Classed-based reality rears its head, though, in *Unreal II: The Awakening*. Paul V. Byrnes describes *Unreal II*'s hero as "John Dalton, a kind of outer space sheriff who's tired of 'patrolling the ass-end of nowhere' and would rather join the marines and go where the action is" (100). Although set in outer space, Byrnes writes that this game is not only multiplayer but also "team and class based" (85).

I find it interesting that class hierarchy is used as a selling trope along with teamwork and the ability to have multiple players, but perhaps I should not be so surprised to see class replicated in cybervisions. Gender

and race certainly show up in the video writer's tool kit for social transformation. Specifically, Byrnes lauds the Xbox live mode of *Unreal II: The
Awakening XMP* for its class differentiation.

> *Awakening*'s *XMP* requires quite a lot of strategy and team coordina-
> tion. Each team's goal is to collect alien artifacts and return them to the
> team's base. To that end, you and your cohorts may also capture spawn
> points, turrets, equipment depots, and vehicles. The classes are well
> differentiated, and because you'll be playing against humans rather than
> the game's idiotic A.I., knowledge of how to use the various weapons
> and their alt-fires actually pays off. (85)

The emphasis on the ability to lie and pass to play Tom Clancy's *Splinter
Cell: Pandora Tomorrow* is emphatic in a lengthy piece in *Xbox Nation*,
which praises the game. In *Passing: When People Can't Be Who They Are,*
author Brooke Kroeger equally emphasizes the stealth involved in successful passing.

> With the props of appearance and talent, passers step out of identities
> dictated by genes, heritage, training, circumstance, or happenstance.
> They must possess the face, voice, skin color, body type, style, and/or
> behavior that defies or confounds easy profiling. Passers stay in char-
> acter no matter what. When the passing is intentional, the passer also
> needs stealth and gumption, cunning, agility, and social conceit.
>
>   Passers curtain off their origins; part-time passers do not own up to
> the other significant involvements in their lives. Passing, in that sense,
> takes guile. Keeping secrets, or at least avoiding certain disclosures, is
> a given in any passing ruse. (8)

Splinter Cell: Pandora Tomorrow, the sequel to *Splinter Cell,* is a highly
successful game that involved, according to Che Chou, "sneaking around
foreign embassies and presidential palaces" (75). *Pandora Tomorrow*
promises more passing via secret identity, taking the player on "an es-
pionage roller coaster" (Chou 76). Chou, in writing about the game, in-
advertently comments on the freedom the class-passer experiences. Like
the real-life class-passer, the virtual game player assumes the role of spy.
"As a spy, you see more of your surroundings, giving you maximum van-
tage for stealth and acrobatics" (78). But spying, like passing of any
kind, is inherently dangerous. If discovered, "spy number two grabs you
from behind and whispers a farewell in your ears before snapping your
neck" (76).

Class is again a selling point for Xbox's *Shellshock: Nam '67*, developed with the "everyman action hero" in mind. Not only is the everyman hero allowed to play Vietnam, so to speak, but *Shellshock* also offers "some of the more unsavory moments during America's long bitter fight: an actual prisoner-torturing mini game and virtual executions" (*Men of Valor* 65).

Digital theory and practice seem to be somewhat at odds. Contrast the embrace of the dystopic in digital video games with Henry Jenkins's notion that "digital theory embraces the utopian imagination . . . as a way of envisioning meaningful change and keeping alive the fluidity that digital media have introduced into many aspects of our social and personal lives" (255). Virtual play allows contact with zones of utopia as well as dystopia.

A useful article in *Electronic Gaming Monthly,* "New School," depicts a sexy blonde schoolteacher in fishnet stockings who breaks down video games into categories such as action games, role-playing games, shooting games, fighting games, stealth games, and weird games. Such categorization helps the player decide which passing zone he or she wishes to engage in. Action games include *Harry Potter and the Prisoner of Azkaban,* which allows players to play Harry, Hermione, or Ron.

As in any game, players can gender-pass or identity-pass in games such as *Harry Potter* or *Onimusha 3,* a samurai action game. I should note here that the most avid gamers are young women, who revel in the chance to gender-pass, adopting masculine names and "user handles" for their personae in role-playing, fighting, and shooting games. In the realm of cyberspace, these young women thus have a chance to act out their aggressions in a declassed arena free from gender expectations, stereotyping, or both, and are free to pursue whatever course of action they feel is most socially expedient. One of the great levelers of the video game is the relative anonymity of the participants; gamers can (and often do) adopt an on-screen identity entirely divorced from the reality of their corporeal existence. While "f2f" (face-to-face) society prescribes certain roles for its inhabitants, cyberspace imposes no such restrictions. The user is thus free to invent herself or himself anew, changing sex, race, cultural identity, and other markers with a few keystrokes. This constant, and consistent, mutability of the real is one of the key attractions of the gaming experience.

Some other action video games that allow all types of passing and identity negotiation include *Spider-Man 2, Narc, Advent Rising,* and *Plague of Darkness. Plague of Darkness* is of interest because it goes beyond class-, gender-, and race-passing. Players of this game enact "ghostly abominations

who roam medieval Europe's plague-ravaged villages, spreading an un-
holy disease" ("New School" 94). *Bloodrayne 2,* which features a super
sexy vampire who hunts down her own siblings, offers players an opportunity to make play out of family dysfunction. Both *Plague of Darkness*
and *Bloodrayne 2,* as well as many other games, allow humans to play
beasts and nonhumans. This feature surpasses perhaps the passing poten-
tial of just about any other venture or venue.

Role-playing games such as *Fable, The Legend of Zelda, X-Men,* and
Jade Empire are but a few examples. The opportunity for a "whole lotta
character-creation freedom" again seems to be a selling point ("New
School" 98). Video games are all about passing and offering myriad opportunities for playing with identity. Perhaps the dullest games are the
shooting games, including *Star Wars: Republic Commando, Doom,* and
Killzone. But even some shooting games allow and encourage passing.
Geist, from Nintendo, offers the "ghostly powers of possession to jump
in and out of your enemies' bodies" ("New School" 100).

The costumes and backgrounds largely facilitate passing in video games.
"Real"-looking costumes as well as "real"-sounding voices abound in the
fighting game *Dead or Alive: Ultimate,* in which "the curvaceous character models look fantastic and the wildly complex (and newly expanded)
stages gleam with absurd amounts of detail . . . plus real-time voice-chat,
online rankings, and organized tournaments will transform an ordinary
ass kicking into full-on public humiliation" ("New School" 106). This
tantalizing interface with the real world of online participation only adds
to the excitement of passing and identity adoption.

Stealth games such as *Starcraft: Ghost* promise to move even closer to
the "real." In *Starcraft: Ghost,* the lead player, Nova, has extraordinary
powers that appeal to the passer in all of us.

"Nova is an elite covert operative called a Ghost," says Producer John
Lagrave. "She was trained from an early age to become a one-woman
army." But anyone can walk softly and carry a big gun—it's Nova's sci-
fi-flavored skills that make her one tough chica. "She was born with
psionic gifts," says Lagrave. "She [also] has a sight ability that allows
her to see lingering footprints . . . or through objects. She has a speed
ability as well. In game, we slow down the world and let Nova operate
at normal speed, which allows her to get past timing puzzles and dodge
incoming fire with ease."
She brings those skills to a war between the terrans ("think space
marines," says Lagrave), zerg ("scary insectoid aliens"), and protoss

("highly advanced psionic aliens, [like] a cross between Jedi and vul-cans"). Fans of the original PC real-time-strategy game *StarCraft* know this war of the worlds all too well—now they can fight the good fight on consoles on a most personal, face-to-face level. ("New School" 108)

The last category discussed in the "New School" article is "weird" games. One of these games returns us to the societal obsession with ce-lebrity and filmmaking. *The Movies* offers a cyberpassing space for those interested in experiencing the lives of movie stars, certainly a safer option than participating in *I Want a Famous Face*. In *The Movies* we find that

being a movie star has its drawbacks—you gotta be in great shape, give up your privacy, and sign an irritating number of autographs. The Hollywood job you really want is studio owner, and designer Peter Molyneux (*Populous, Theme Park*) understands this. To put it in true Hollywood terms, *The Movies* is *The Sims* meets *The Player*. You run a movie studio from the early days of cinema right though 2010. You select scripts, design sets, direct the cast and crew, and deal with diva actors and their entourages. "[You] basically experience anything you've ever read about Hollywood—from stars' bad behavior and expensive turkeys to meteoric rises to stardom and surprise box-office success," Molyneux says. ("New School" 112)

Cyberpassers are not unlike real-life passers, regardless of the type of video game. As Brooke Kroeger reminds us, "passing stories allow us to see which aspects of identity seem to be fixed and unchangeable. . . . For those of us looking in, such stories allow us a gauge where we stand per-sonally and as a society in the wider subject of identity itself" (9). The wonder of creating multiple selves is aided in the cyberworld by effects that can erase the world we know as "reality" and the creation of com-plete other worlds. One reviewer of *SSX 3*, for example, says of the game, "I can't think of another game that has presented such a complete 'world.' From the way that everything is a part of one big mountain, to little de-tails like BIG Radio, this game really made me feel like I was a part of something cool" ("Annual Awards Special" 49).

Video games find and chart a space where "private persons are an il-lusion," as Deleuze and Guattari put it (264). They allow participants the feeling that they are not slaves of the social machine or bodies that are disciplined by reality and its social rules. They are by nature both utopic, dystopic, and something quite extraordinary: places of displacement, places of passing. Corporeal real passing is replaced by narratives of cybermimicry, in which physiological and social rules do not apply. Video games can be seen as passing machines, in a way, but one must remember that those cyber experiences are not real.

Reality, ironically perhaps, is more likely to pop up and flummox the class-passer in filmed fictions such as *Maid in Manhattan* (Wayne Wang, 2002). This Cinderella-like tale revolved around the ethnic- and class-passing of a Latina maid, played by Jennifer Lopez. An upper-class senatorial candidate, played by Ralph Fiennes, falls for the maid when she tries on a very wealthy woman's dress and he sees her. It is a story that has been told so many times in Hollywood films: a couple who are different in class status meet and encounter obstacles; eventually the class-passer is "outed" by events and must explain himself or herself to the other. The fairy-tale quality of such films is undercut, however, by their messages about social class and its grim realities; the difference in ethnicities further complicates this film. Lopez's maid has not experienced the comforts of the white middle or upper class.

Her routines as a lower-class Latina woman are painful and well rendered. Many reviewers had issues with the completely unbelievable plot. Most find it outrageous that this woman can effectively use her charm and plot points in the narrative to class-pass effectively and maneuver around her identity as a Latina woman into the world of the very distinctly classed politician. Of course the plot is preposterous. Of course it seems highly unlikely, if not impossible. But given the phantasmal dreams of all sorts of passing in video games and elsewhere, why are critics so incredibly hard on a fairy-tale class-passing film such as *Maid in Manhattan?* Could it be that they would rather not see Jennifer Lopez, even in 2002, achieve upward mobility? Why reject utopias, no matter how far-fetched, in celluloid? Must we live in this world and not class-pass in any fictive world?

Classing the Body: Cash-Passing and Class "Mashup"

Fantasies of body modification equal or better the popular culture fantasies of class mobility. These fantasies are deeply related in ways that are as complex as they are opaque. With the rise of the celebrity class system and the rituals of body culture, the impossibility of fully class-passing is as wildly apparent as is the impossibility of having the perfect body. As Paul Fussell notes, "it would be sad to calculate the energy wasted in both pursuits" (170). The strain and effort millions spend, whether on steroid popping by bodybuilders, pain toleration by the tattooed, or the masquerade of class-passing by Oprah, Donald Trump, Roseanne Barr, Martha Stewart, and Britney Spears, is all done in the name of celebrity. All are wildly successful, yes, but these are actually cash-passers more than class-passers, because their roots in lower classes will always show, as will their efforts to class-pass.

Bizarrely, in a world in which everything revolves around cash, Britney Spears is treated with far more reverence than, say, Judy Dench. Class matters, but cash matters more. Oddly, the narratives of celebrity class rise always allude to the working-class origins of megacelebrities such as Britney Spears. Spears's working-class roots are frequently alluded to in her interviews and endless profiles. The same is true for Oprah Winfrey,

Donald Trump, Roseanne Barr, and Martha Stewart. Their roots show, their striving shows. They are proud of their striving. It is a badge of honor. But ironically, this striving undercuts the illusion of full-class stature, just as the massive muscles of bodybuilders betray the number of hours they spend in the gym and the torturous regimes they put themselves through to attain standards of perfection that are themselves unattainable. Asked whether she worried that her image promotes feelings of inadequacy in young people already plagued by self-esteem issues, Britney told Steven Daly that she considers herself a role model, even while admitting that the role model is itself something unattainable. Spears responds diplomatically. "When people see things on TV that they can't do," she ventures, "that should make them want to go out there and make something of themselves. That's how I looked at it" (51).

As a cash-passer rather than a class-passer, it is very important that Britney constantly remind us of her roots. The illusion that Britney Spears is a self-made woman is very important to uphold the masquerade of cash-passing. "They think people put me together. I come up with the ideas," states Spears in a caption over a photo spread that shows Britney's various fantasy outfits from 2000 to 2004, attire reminiscent of Liberace's early glam look of the 1950s. The three-page article indulges the viewer in sixteen Britney fantasies ("Red Carpet" 12–17). The vertical placement of the photographs is reminiscent of test tubes holding bodies, not unlike the cover art of eighties punk musical group X-Ray Spex's album *Germ Free Adolescents* (1978). X-Ray Spex's lyrics, such as those from the pop song "Identity," railed against cookie-cutter identity fantasies, just like those Britney Spears projects. X-Ray Spex waged an explosive Marxist critique that railed against materialism, but more specifically, the group railed against corporate popular cultures' insistence that young women deny their individualism and model themselves after airbrushed images of impossibility. Punk rock, often mishistoricized as a movement that was simply antiestablishment, was indeed deeply humanist in nature. The values espoused by punk bands such as the Slits, the Bust Tetras, the Modettes, the Gang of Four, and the Raincoats and, more recently, post-punk bands such as Le Tigre are anticorporate culture and anticelebrity culture. Conspicuous consumption and celebrity are not things to aspire to in songs such as "Spend Spend Spend" and "Instant Hit" (Slits album *Cut*, 1979). Granted, these groups were a counterculture, but the twenty-first century's full embrace of corporate-driven celebrity product, such as Britney Spears and Donald Trump as role models, is truly frightening.

Young girls aspire to actually *be* Britney, and young girls find Donald Trump, because of his newfound success on *The Apprentice,* sexy and cool—even a desirable mate. Trump was only mildly teased by late-night talk show hosts for his recent marriage to a young woman in her twenties.

At the same time, the fanatical and widespread mass cultural embrace of body culture threatens to replace or at least displace dated notions of class hierarchy, as well as myths and ambitions of class mobility. Class mobility has either merged or been obliterated by body culture. "Because all men are *not* created equal," shouts an advertisement for a no-impact elliptical trainer, the SportsArt 807 Elliptical (41). The rhetoric of class rise here is borrowed and renarrated to fit the new body class system. The energy spent on the pursuit of mastery of the corporeal class system displaces the energy that might go into class mobility or corporate rise if that were still an achievable goal in these times. The pursuit of money is eyed with suspicion in muscle-building culture, as if time spent making money is precious time spent away from the gym. An unnamed writer in "Titus Talks," a question-and-answer column penned by bodybuilder Craig Titus, disparages Titus.

> I've been a hardcore bodybuilder for five years and I'm a devout member of several Internet message boards. It seems like every week the boards are full of your yapping about all your new contracts. I mean no disrespect, Craig, but come on, you're talkin' like a lyin' bitch! No one in this sport has that many contracts! You need to come clean now, or I'll flame you until your fat gut explodes into a virtual mass of intestines all over the 'Net. You've been warned. ("Titus Talks" 370, 372)

Titus responds to the writer's attack, or class-trashing, with a defense of his right to make a living, ending with an open invitation for yet more publicity and wealth.

> You've gotta calm down, man! You need to understand that I do not lie or feel the need to boast about my accomplishments. I'm just proud and feel very blessed. Don't spread hate on a bodybuilder just because he can make a living. That is something that should be respected, because doing so is not easy, my friend. Kelly and I are very blessed and thankful for what we have, but you should know that we have worked really hard to get where we are.
>
> The truth is that we do have quite a few contracts. Right now, we've got Pinnacle, Cytodyne, Hardbodies Home Gym, APT Pro Wrist Strap, Oxygen and MD. Kelly also writes for Bodybuilding.com. After this

season, I'll be looking for an agreement with whoever wants to sign me
to a publication deal. (372)

Class-trashing and trash talking seem central to bodybuilding culture.
Vocal and verbal jousting is perhaps necessary in a hierarchy in which
body perfection is measurable not just with the scale and the tape measure but by means of ever-mutating standards of bodily perfection that
are subjective in nature. Ironically, the same muscle magazines designed
to help set the standards for the perfect male body resort to digital images of massive sculpted bodies such as those in an ad for Full Impact Bolt,
a supplement that promises to aid in recovery from weight training. Even
the ad notes that "stringent criteria of success can be *confusing at best,*
but working out isn't rocket science, so why is it so difficult to compile a
formula that is built to work?" (286–87; emphasis mine).

A cover story in *Muscular Development* about Jimmy Canyon, written by Ron Harris, attempts to compile such a formula. The black-and-
white images of Canyon show him in postures of contortion and pain with
a body Leni Riefenstahl would drool over. Jimmy Canyon has the "best
abs in the world" (214), according to Harris. Two photographs of Canyon are especially interesting because they look like depictions of Jesus
Christ on the cross, the only difference being that this Christlike figure is
hanging from a bar and suffers excruciating pain not at the hands of the
Romans but in his own quest for perfection.

Bodies in *Muscular Development* are machines in pain, but perfection
is unobtainable. The writers are as brutally judgmental of the bodybuilders
as the bodybuilders are of themselves. Flex Wheeler, for example, disapproves of the amazing body of Ronny Rockel.

> They call him Ronny "The Rock" Rockel. I'm sure he deserves that
> name from somewhere, but not at this show. He was carrying far too
> much water, but you can tell this is a guy who has a body type that can
> come in extremely hard if he wanted to. If he was in shape, he would
> have definitely hurt some people's feelings. Ronny is a short, stocky guy,
> but his pecs, guns, quads and back are very big. I would like to see him
> dial it in better. He'll place higher then. (177)

Once again, the impossible standards of bodybuilding mimic the *impossibility* of full class-passing. The makers of V12 Turbo, "the most
versatile ergogenic and physique altering product," do not even use a photograph of a ripped male body to sell this product. Instead, the ad sports
an imposing-looking V12 engine. Consumers are encouraged to think of

themselves as nonhuman. But even with this celebration of "form and function at the highest level of perfection," the machinelike body is, as the advertisement admits, informed by "a mental concept of the *unobtainable*" (40–41; emphasis mine).

Another product, Off Cycle, promises to build "almost freakish muscle mass!" (21). Freakishness is embraced here—whatever it takes to obtain the unobtainable. This is a virtual reality more hyperreal than digital games. It is absurdly weird in its quest for an unreal body. The call to the body class-passer is a call to the submissive end of the sadomasochist contract as much as it is a call toward the primal, the feral, animal Other as it-he is displayed in an ad for Animal hard-core training packs. Animal's advertisement displays a huge bodybuilder in a cell, perhaps a jail cell. He looks away from the viewer, head down, perhaps ashamed of his incongruently "perfect" body. The ad copy is cleverly voiced, as if it comes from an inner drill sergeant, the subconscious tormentor-coach of the faceless bodybuilder.

> "Squat til You Puke." You stand alone, ten plates in the hole. It's you versus the weight. You're thinking, "I'm gonna get friggin' crushed." You're thinking, "I'm not gonna get up." But you will. Yeah, you'll puke. Yeah, it'll be hard getting off the crapper the next couple days. But it'll be worth it, cuz when there's chalk on your hands and sweat on your back, there's no better place in the world. This is pain. This is animal. Can you handle it? (16)

Self-punishment is a necessary ingredient toward class rise in the schema of the body cult class system. Elsa Kay, sounding a bit like the voice of *Ilsa, She Wolf of the SS* (from Don Edmond's 1974 trash-film classic) tells her readers to find their inner coach in a nasty sadistic voice that appeals to basic masochism.

> I mean punishing yourself if you don't show up to the gym. Talk to yourself like a coach, not like a guy who would rather sleep another nine minutes. When your lazy self thinks, "I'm so tired," make your inner coach respond, "Get over it, wimp." Throw in some obscenities to make it even more authentic.
>
> And penalize yourself if you stray from the routine. Let's say you plan to run three miles on the treadmill, and you wimp out on mile two. Your inner coach should make you do four the next day. Or lift more weights. Or take a cardio-funk class and make a fool of yourself. Hey, the inner coach can be ruthless. (41)

Similarly, the copy in an advertisement for Xvest, an adjustable weighted vest alludes to sadomasochistic bondage, specifically those fetishes that have to do with immobilizing the masochistic sex partner. "By making basic motions more difficult your body requires more muscle fibers to be called into action" (63). But it is never enough. No amount of time and pain endured at the gym will ever be enough—this is evident in the numerous ads for plastic surgery, sex drive enhancement products, supplements such as Balls 2 the Wall, pills for penis enlargement, and the muscle-building magazines themselves, such as *Muscular Development,* which announces, "We have the winning formula" (418). Interspersed with these advertisements are numerous articles defining the use of anabolic steroids. After a lengthy disclaimer, competitive bodybuilder Dave Palumbo informs the reader just how to use steroids, in what combination, and so forth, in the aptly titled column, "The Anabolic Freak." Another columnist, John Romano, argues that steroids should be legal because birth control pills are actually steroids: "How, as a parent, are you going to tell junior it's okay for his little 15-year-old sister to take steroids (birth control pills) so she can have recreational sex without getting pregnant, but he can't take steroids—ever—to help him become bigger, leaner, faster or stronger?" (242).

Shocked by George W. Bush's state-of-the-union address (in which he declared war on steroids), Romano is himself greatly distressed by the government's intrusion in steroid use.

> Obviously, steroids have been alive and kicking on the front burner of government action. If not, why would the President feel compelled to call our attention to a "problem" today, when sport has had rules in place to combat them for years? Why mention it now? Is the "problem" today any worse than it was when the President co-owned the Texas Rangers? Where was the big call to arms when he was a team owner? That is but one of many questions that begs to be answered. But, more important than that, will Bush's declaration affect us? (242)

Who exactly is the "us" referred to in the final sentence of Romano's rant? The old class rules do not apply in the world of bodybuilding. But some advertisements specifically summon older notions of class and their stations. An advertisement for Endless Pool, for example, stresses its upper-classedness. "The elegant solution to crowded pools, difficult schedules, flip-turns and staying fit. Now you can swim whenever you like, on your own schedule, at your own perfect pace. No traveling, no crowded pools" (49).

"Uncrowded" pools offer an elegant class-based solution, but Brave Soldier, a shaving product line, is made for "all the rough and tough guys out there" (Wilson 29). The Art of Shaving product line mentioned in the same article by Stevie Wilson appears to mimic the name of a book corporate climbers read, *The Art of War,* and King of Shaves uses all but obsolete royalty class nostalgia in naming its product line. Perhaps unsurprising, an ad for a gun manufacturer, EAA Corporation, uses an image from Leonardo da Vinci's famous *Vitruvian,* displaying the anatomy of the human male, to sell guns "starting at $469" (17).

We are witnessing a sort of class "mashup" in a society undergoing a drastic change from a system that once celebrated pluralism to one that now worships the cash-laden individual at the expense of the citizenry. Country music and tattoo culture, once considered lower-working-class markers, are now part of the fabric of all classes. Celebrities brag about their tattoos, as do people of all ages, races, and classes. Country music, once considered the mark of trash culture, is embraced as much by the cognoscenti as it is by the masses, as if the entire country decided to go slumming. But this cultural move is neither a sign of slumming nor a return to pluralism. It is a mass-media dictate to which everyone seems to respond as just so many lambs to the slaughter. Class is no longer about whether one is educated or listens to classical music—those things are not class markers. They are used as demographics to sell products, yes, but they are no longer strictly class markers. If anything, these changes mark a faux egalitarianism. Visit a tattoo parlor, and one can pick up a copy of *Redneck World, Tattoo,* or *Skin/Art.* There, one is likely to see a middle-class sophisticate just as much as a lower-class worker.

In much the same fashion, Wal-Mart stocks everything from *Town and Country* to *Special Weapons.* Our new pluralism is based on greed and selfishness. An ad for Black Radiance cosmetics says it all: "It's all about you!" (63). Nevertheless, class mixing, or class mashing, is undoubtedly cool, as evidenced in an *Essence* profile of the clothing style of Mary J. Blige. Blige is lauded for her "elegant" mashup of "girl from Yonkers influences" with "high fashion" ("Mary J. Blige" 62). Not only is class erased, but so is race in this description of Blige.

> "What's appealing about the way she dresses is that it's so eclectic: Couture meets sex kitten meets urban chic," says stylist and judge Timothy Snell, who has worked with Angela Bassett, Whitney Houston and Tisha Campbell Martin. "She has blended these worlds and made them her own—beautifully." Snell appreciates Mary's evolution over the

last few years. "Her wardrobe has lightened up, her color choices are brighter, and the silhouettes are much more feminine," he notes. "She's emerged confidently as a true celebrity fashionist." (62)

Celebrities are just like us, at least according to the media. So we should not be surprised that women are blithely told in one article that their body type is just like that of Halle Berry. Kacy Duke proclaims that the body of Halle Berry is indeed attainable: "Many of my clients relate to Halle's body type because she has hips and a butt. They see her shape as both beautiful and attainable" (64).

I find that thinking Halle Berry's tiny, lithe, hip-free body type is attainable (by more than a handful of people) is as absurd as thinking that Audrey Hepburn's or Calista Flockheart's body types are attainable. Body obsessions are the special topic of an issue of *Jane*. In a bizarre ad, *Jane*'s editors "apologize to you if you have ever felt weird or ugly after viewing these pages. . . . We would like you, the customer, to be aware that we do make every effort to support every woman in her quest not to covet, envy or deify any other woman and/or that woman's body" (69).

This letter-ad is cleverly postmodern in its direct address to the viewer. It appears to be an article in the *New York Times*, rephotographed for the ad in *Jane*. Absurdly, a piece in the same issue, "Flesh Survey," states that "1,500 of you [readers] copped to everything from puking up your food to loving your monster trunks in *Jane*'s first ever Flesh Survey" (20). Questions include "Are you generally happy with your body?" (20) and "Is your favorite body part the same thing you get complimented on?" (21).

Products such as Airbrush Legs and Sally Hansen's Airbrush Makeup for all Skins are interspersed with an article by Michael Thompson in which Kate Winslet protests the fakery of her airbrushed and digitally enhanced photographs. "I do not look like that," insists Kate. "And more importantly I do not desire to look like that" (110). The blatantly airbrushed and digitally enhanced photographs of Kate Winslet in this issue of *Jane*, both on the cover and throughout the Thompson article, however, further highlight the absurdity of this article.

Confusing the issue further is a photo spread in *Jane* by David Ferrura, "We've All Gone Insane," which features a photograph of an in vitro fetus with the caption, "at that weight, she'll never be a model" (130). The Ferrura photo spread, a heartfelt critique of the body class system, is undercut by ads for skin products that promise a digital airbrushed look. The many photographs of models thin enough to be heroin junkies spread throughout the same issue of *Jane*, not to mention the "minute-a-day

method to a perfect shape" article advertised on the cover, further undercut and confuse the issue. Ferrura is correct. We have gone insane.

The mind-set of *Jane* seems just as insane as that of *Muscular Development*. *Essence* also has mixed messages about class, body culture, celebrity, and passing. "Celebrity-Inspired Makeover," in *Essence,* actually
revolves around making one celebrity (model Tighisti Amahazion) look
like *another* celebrity, Alicia Keys.

Celebrities passing as other celebrities? Yes, we have gone insane, but
Amahazion is thrilled with her transformation into an Alicia Keys look-
alike: "I love the versatility of her music and her faithfulness to Afrocentric
style" (86). This kind of passing is not so much about upward mobility
or even celebrity class-passing; rather it borders on identity-passing because both the passer and the passee share celebrity class status. Oddly
enough at the beginning of the same issue of *Essence,* editor-in-chief Diane
Weathers promises sensible stories "about ordinary women who've climbed
out of poverty and into prosperity" (30). True enough, this issue contains
not only profiles of businesswomen who have achieved upward mobility
but also articles about how to get out of credit-card debt. Complicating
the message, however, is an advertisement for the American Express Blue
Cash credit card, which promises, "It pays you rent for living in your
wallet" (99). Far from paying you rent, credit cards can get you into the
debt that keeps you from ever achieving upward mobility—that same
upward mobility the editor-in-chief of *Essence* experienced, for example.

Class-passing is a messy yet celebrated affair, and race and ethnicity,
of course, complicate it further. An advertisement for the U.S. Virgin Islands is a good case in point. The copy in this ad urges the reader to "explore a little further our rich African American heritage" (191). This rather
crass call to the reaffirmation of blackness strikes me as a bit confusing.
Although the ad says you can "spot your heritage on a trail," you have
to wonder how many African Americans actually trace their heritage
through the Virgin Islands (191). Most accounts of slave passages and port
of entries do not revolve around this particular vacation spot, but ad copy
is not designed to appeal to history. It is designed to appeal to fantasies
of upward mobility, and finding one's heritage is a specifically classed trope
the travel industry often uses. Ireland depends on it. So does Aer Lingus.

Although truth is displaced for some commercial purposes, it is invoked
as a reality claim for others. Thus *Redemption* (Vondie Curtis Hall, 2004),
a made-for-television movie, is advertised as being "based on a true story."
This narrative, starring Jamie Foxx, appears to be all about the celebration

of a successful class-passer whose upward mobility is displayed as he moves from "gangster" to "death row inmate" to "Nobel Peace Prize nominee" (145). The film is sold as a gangsta-made-good narrative. Indeed, *Redemption* is based on the true story of Crips gang founder Stan "Tookie" Williams. When a professor (Lynn Whitfield) who wants to write a book about the Crips goes to see Williams (Foxx) in prison, the two "begin a friendship that will have a significant effect upon the lives of millions of young people" (*The Movie Insider*). Gang membership, in the world of *Redemption,* is viewed as a stepping stone to successful class-passing and general legitimacy in society. In *Redemption,* tried-and-true messages regarding class mobility are mixed up, or mashed up, with newer celebrity-informed or gang-related class-rising tropes.

Whether for race heritage or workout wear, the signs of class struggle are apparent in the language we use to sell products that appeal to our need for social mobility. Thus a Russell Athletic advertisement asks, "Are you Russell Athletic material?," noting difference in class when it comes to running ability: "One man's workout is another man's warm-up" (55).

Our confusing state of class as a mashup, coupled with our embrace of celebrity- and cash-classing, is evident in the prevalence of rants and raves against those who attempt to class-pass. A good place to locate these rants is in the letters-to-the-editor column in magazines such as *Sister 2 Sister.* "No Crazy Fan" writes,

> Fans in the U.S. are so crazy in love with these celebrities until they go off the deep end. Whitney's Christmas CD may be wonderful but fans have to show these celebrities what they will and will not tolerate. I've had enough of [Whitney Houston's] and Bobby's shenanigans and their circle of friends who dismiss their irrational and unprofessional behavior as being picked on. . . . I refuse to fork over my hard earned $75 for a concert ticket to have someone: show up two hours late, be a no-show, excessive drug use, statutory rape, molestation of a child, shooting up a nightclub, and the list goes on and on and on for these people who just happen to make mega millions. Our community, the Black one, looks to the rest of the world like the majority of us don't even care what, how, when, and where. Do we? . . . Today, we live in an "anything goes" society. Gangster rap artists can use all kinds of profanity and denigrating terms in their songs, all in the name of what they endured in the ghetto. A therapist can help with that. Puhleeze!! I have no problem with them recording their music but I don't want to hear it on TV, period. Play it on certain radio stations and be done with it. . . .

Forty years ago some of these celebrities' careers would've been over the day after a negative article came out. Considering their self-indulgent behavior, it would be rightfully so. (94–95)

The flaunting of wealth was once a no-no under the old rules of class. Today's celebrities not only flaunt wealth but also name themselves after it. Cash Money, 50 Cent, and any number of other artists now use monikers that court or display wealth. Often their songs mix tales of the projects with tales of bling and the good life of trash and flash. Jamie Foster Brown interviewed celebrity tennis star Serena Williams, who seems positively blasé about her $60 million Nike deal.

> *Jamie:* Let's talk about your endorsement deal with Nike. Congratulations!
> *Serena:* Thank you.
> *Jamie:* The deal is reportedly a $60 million deal. What does the deal include?
> *Serena:* I don't get into details with it.
> *Jamie:* You're not supposed to do that?
> *Serena:* Yeah.
> *Jamie:* Does that make you the richest female athlete?
> *Serena:* That's what they say. (75)

She seems almost as if she's bored with the talk of money, so assured is she of her celebrity class status. In a similar vein, Serena downplays the work she puts into her hard and pumped-up body.

> *Jamie:* Were you always built the way you are or were you skinny, then blossomed?
> *Serena:* No. I was just looking at some pictures of when I was really young. I had diesel arms. I was like, "oh my." I don't really work out so much on my upper body. (71)

Somehow, I just don't buy it. Serena Williams's upper body is as finely sculpted as a bodybuilder's. In an interesting twist, interviewer Niki Turner finds herself answering questions in an interview with celebrity singer Avant when he demonstrates his boredom with talking about celebrity.

> *Avant:* Are you looking for somebody, baby?
> *Niki:* (Laughing)
> *Avant:* I had to put that "private room" on there. I had to put that baby on there.

Niki: Okay, but back to you.

Avant: See, now wait a minute. Why does this interview gotta be about me?

Niki: It is about you!!

Avant: I can switch it around.

Niki: No, you're the celebrity.

Avant: I understand but right now, you're my celebrity. Wait a minute!! I'mma break it down like my man said, you are the prototype. (49)

One has to ask whether Avant is bored with celebrity, tired of talking about his personal life, or just playing the trickster by turning around the interview.

Manipulating the discourse in a magazine profile is far easier, as evidenced in an article about Christina Norman, president of VH1, the subject of Karen Halliburton's "Who Does She Think She Is?" published in *Sister 2 Sister.* First and foremost, Norman is described as successful. Halliburton opens her profile with a definition of success: "Success. Webster's describes it as the attainment of wealth, favor, or eminence" (28). Here we see no mention of class or upward mobility, yet these parts of success are inscribed in the description of success as laid bare by Norman via Webster's. In describing the actual work that Norman performed to become VH1's president, Halliburton summarizes, "Girlfriend gave a booster shot to the network's image, re-energizing the once challenged VH1" (28). We find out that Norman moved through the ranks from senior vice president of marketing and on-air promotion for MTV, MTV2, and MTV.com. She launched the highest-rated MTV series, *The Osbournes,* for example. Norman's fabulous marketing skills paid off. Now, like most celebrities, she uses yoga to relieve her stress. Hers is an old-fashioned story of class mobility accented by race mobility. Halliburton summarizes, "No, doubt, Christina is a media maven to peeps. Amazing? Yes. Mega-talented? Yes. Empowering leader? Yes. Christina Norman is a positive ray beaming the light of success in her path" (31).

But fame always has a price, as shown in the stories of Beyoncé's stalker nightmare, P. Diddy's lawsuit by a former chauffeur, and the reported injury of Halle Berry on the set of Pitof's *Catwoman* (2004) after one on the set of Mathieu Kassovitz's *Gothika* (2003).

One of the harshest costs any celebrity pays is the almost inevitable appearance in a "Where Are They Now?" article, typified in an example of the genre from the April 3–10, 2004, issue of *TV Guide.* The title of the essay itself is a dead giveaway to the price of fame and celebrity. Once you class-pass over into the realm of celebrity, you are subject to the rules of celebrity class-passing. One of the first rules is to maintain your public image, stay in the public eye, no matter what. "Where Are They Now?" suggests that they (celebrity has-beens) are no longer someplace. That place is a class called celebrity. No matter how successful the postcelebrity is, he or she is perceived as a has-been. For example, Eriq La Salle, once a star on *ER*, is directing episodes of the new *Twilight Zone* series, as well as working on other projects. Nevertheless, La Salle, just by virtue of showing up in a "Where Are They Now?" column, is perceived as lacking in celebrity cachet.

Barbara Feldon, once a star of *Get Smart* as Agent 99, is similarly punished for not being more available and not being in the public eye. Celebrityhood is a full-time job: one cannot just walk away from it and expect to stay in the limelight. You've got to work it, 24/7. In "real life," Feldon has been successful. She has written novels and essays, but somehow she will always have to apologize for no longer being Agent 99 on *Get Smart,* a television show that ran from 1965 to 1970, as well as in reruns for a few more decades. "Where Are They Now?" articles and books act as nags, public nags, tracking down erstwhile celebrities and urging them to return to the public eye.

One of the reasons for the great success of reality television is that the celebrities featured on it allow total access to their personal lives. Round the clock, hour by hour, they lose any sense of personal space and behave as celebrities. But these are celebrities that will do anything to feed their public. In ABC's *Extreme Makeover,* instant reality television celebrities undergo intensive, intrusive, and dangerous plastic surgery. These class-jumpers hurdle their way into the celebrity class by virtue of their willingness to do more than pass. The intrusiveness demanded by the program's audience is demonstrated in a profile called *"Extreme Makeover"* in a magazine called *Reality TV.* For example, John Clooney, a video game designer, underwent a chin implant, nose job, eye surgery, fat injections in his face, and liposuction in the neck. He also endured teeth whitening and bonding. "I used to be an introvert," he says, "but now I'm outgoing. I'm just a happier person" (131).

Extreme Makeover gives us some insight into the manner in which class- and body-passing, not to mention celebrity-passing, have been accelerated and manipulated into instant mini versions of Horatio Alger tales and, more closely, Cinderella tales. Indeed, the Web site for the series precisely delineates the impact of *Extreme Makeover* on the American public consciousness.

> Following nationwide open casting calls and over 10,000 written applications, the lucky individuals are chosen for a once-in-a-lifetime chance to participate in *Extreme Makeover*. These men and women are given a truly Cinderella-like experience: A real life fairy tale in which their wishes come true, not just to change their looks, but their lives and destinies. This magic is conjured through the skills of an "Extreme Team," including the nation's top plastic surgeons, eye surgeons and cosmetic dentists, along with a talented team of hair and makeup artists, stylists and personal trainers, led by an on-camera *Extreme Makeover* expert. This season will feature more "news you can use" tips about fashion, hair and makeup for the home viewers. Each self-contained episode will feature two people, seen first in their "before" phase, then as they undergo their various procedures, and finally, in a climactic unveiling—"the after"—when the candidates reveal their new selves to their families and friends.

To up the ante, ABC has begun coupling the extreme makeover concept with a televised wedding, as couples are "transformed" before our eyes and then married on national television. Significantly, while we are allowed to watch the plastic surgery on the groom's face and body without much obstruction (even in the operating room, where the violence to the body that the surgery represents, both physically and metaphorically, is displayed as a kind of "splatter" side show), the bride's face is hidden beneath a thick veil after her surgery. Our view of her countenance is obscured until the last possible moment, when, after a barrage of commercials, we are presented with what the show describes as "the reveal," the first view of her face. The marriage follows immediately, and the viewing audience is presumably satisfied with the spectacle of instantaneous transformation that has been presented.

Americans obsess with before and after photographs, constantly judging one another and retooling the impossible standards of beauty and personhood to unrealistic and dangerous standards, as unobtainable as those set by bodybuilding magazines or by the obsessed celebrity wannabes of *I Want a Famous Face*. The before and after photographs inevitably suggest success, but they also imply failure. No one can be perfect in a world in which perfection is beyond imagining. Weight loss, rhinoplasty, breast augmentation, cheek implants, butt implants, hair removal, hair implants:

all these things imply failure. The best one can look after an extreme makeover is the best that can be done with the particular individual.

Sure, contestants on *Extreme Makeover* can look "better," but what exactly is "best," and how do we define perfection? The nebulous class-based obsession with the body leaves us ultimately as confused by our standards, or lack thereof, as did our old-fashioned class system of hierarchies based on money, power, birth, and job description. The *Extreme Makeover* celebrity is never a successful pass because the before picture is always there to remind us of who they "really" are—just as Martha Stewart is always associated with the photograph of her modest first home, her "lower" birth, her humble beginnings. The body will wear out, just as the roots of the class-passer will always show.

Part of any "passing" narrative is the reveal. Gender-passing narratives, such as *The Ballad of Little Jo* (Maggie Greenwald, 1993), asks the viewer simply to wait until the cowgirl who has been passing as a man is found out, even in death. Similarly, the passing story of *The Human Stain* (Robert Benton, 2003) would hold no interest without the inevitable "reveal." In this film, based on the Philip Roth novel of the same name, a Jewish academic, Coleman Silk, is revealed to be actually an African American. A connected story about Wentworth Miller, who plays the young version of the lead in *The Human Stain,* is also a race-passer, if by only the nature of his mixed ethnic heritage. Wentworth is of African American, Jamaican, German, English, Russian, Dutch, French, Syrian, and Lebanese descent. Whether he is made to pass in the film or if he is "passing" in life is difficult to determine. His mixed-race status always has the narrative of the "reveal" inherently attached to his identity if only because of the American obsession with race definitions. Anthony Hopkins, by all accounts a white Anglo-Saxon, passes as the older Silk in *The Human Stain,* although this act of passing is never convincing to the audience.

Perhaps the inevitable slippage of the masquerade of identity moves people to mark their own identities with tattoos, for example. The most sought after tattoo artists are those who promise one-of-a-kind designs, such as Chris Blinston of Omaha, Nebraska. Tattoo artists who can promise "realism" are also highly touted. It seems ironic that uniqueness is used to mark difference, to insist on a lack of passing, when it really only reinforces the nature of passing inherent in identity itself. Branding, tattooing, piercing, and all sorts of body manipulations are all the rage, as are phantasmal hair colors and pierced genitalia. But nothing says "I'm worried that I'm like everybody else" quite like these drastic invasive measures.

Andy Warhol, by his own admission a "deeply superficial person," was obsessed with celebrity for much of his career and is often quoted as saying, "In the future, everyone will be famous for fifteen minutes." In 1979 Warhol modified his own dictum, noting that "my prediction from the sixties finally came true: 'In the future everyone will be famous for fifteen minutes.' I'm bored with that line. I never use it anymore. My new line is, 'In fifteen minutes everybody will be famous'" (*The Quotations Page* Web site). But perhaps Warhol did not go far enough. Perhaps in the future, the classes themselves will be divided between those who are celebrities and those who are not. Seem far-fetched? Recall for a moment the once-futuristic vision of Elio Petri's *The Tenth Victim* (1965), in which almost everyone in a future society signs up to play in a celebrity death match, the results of which are, of course, televised. Critic Sean Axmaker notes,

> Long before reality shows took over the TV airwaves and violent parodies like [Daniel Minahan's 2001 film] *Series 7* and [Kinji Fukasaku's 2000 film] *Battle Royale* hit international screens, Elio Petri made [*The Tenth Victim*, a brilliant] social satire of a future in which the bored, the ambitious, and the just plain violent can sign up for a deadly game of cat and mouse. "The Big Hunt is necessary as a social safety valve," explains one TV personality. "Why control births when we can control deaths?" (*The Tenth Victim* Web site)

Petri, like Jean-Luc Godard in his dystopic masterpiece *Alphaville* (1965), ultimately prefers a romanticized humanist twist, in which two people seemingly destined to kill one another wind up falling hopelessly in love instead. The futuristic visions of *Alphaville* and *The Tenth Victim* now seem, juxtaposed with such programs as *Survivor* and *Big Brother,* to belong to an earlier and gentler era. The possibility of genuine romance always offsets violence in these films; in the current era, the protagonists of today's "reality shows" have no such assurance. Although state-sanctioned murder is not yet a part of the repertoire of today's crop of reality shows, violence to the body and the psyche is a routine part of most reality programs, from *Fear Factor* to *My Big Fat Obnoxious Fiancé.* The entire function of the "elimination round" common to most reality television game shows has become a fetishized moment of tribal rejection, in everything from *Survivor* to Donald Trump's ritualistic incantation "you're fired" on *The Apprentice.* When *Alphaville* and *The Tenth Victim* were initially released, no one thought of them as anything other than social satire and criticism, when in fact they were acts of prognostication. They accurately forecast the current televisual trend toward real-life, hyper-surviellantly documented self-humiliation and ritualized violence. Have we become so obsessed with celebrity that we are willing to give up our lives for it? Will we readily surrender, for the sake of a momentary flicker of notoriety, our faces, our identities, our lives, and our friends? When will someone who undergoes plastic surgery for a celebrity television show die under the knife? Is it not only a matter of time before this happens or before someone is killed or permanently disabled while performing any one of the many exceedingly dangerous stunts on *Fear Factor*? Is it not only a matter of time before we are classed not by our class status, such as it is, but rather by our celebrity status? Has that time already arrived?

Our classed mashup of a culture is undergoing a rich discussion about identity itself via its rituals, its obsession with celebrity, mobility, and all the identity markers that we are familiar with: race, gender, sexuality, age, and so on. But many questions remain. By omitting class from the discussions about race, gender, sexuality, age, and other issues, we have obfuscated all the ways in which class enters into the identity equation. In fact we need to rethink identity politics with class and class-passing in mind. We must return to basic questions. We must rethink traditional notions of class and their hierarchies. We must ask tough questions. Is race a form of class? Is gender treated as class? Is sexuality really a class distinction? How is age treated or received as a class? Is nationality and ethnicity class-based? What avenues can we explore in looking at class from the position of the class-passer? The cash-passer? The class-mashup? Most important, how do we reinvest our theories of popular culture with richer and fuller discussions of class? And how do we reinterpret class, keeping in mind our postmodern identity shifts and the changes in our global economic systems? How are we to reimagine class mobility? What are we to make of class-passing, and how are we to underscore enough that, indeed, *class matters?*

WORKS CITED AND CONSULTED
INDEX

Works Cited and Consulted

Adorno, T. W. "Culture Industry Reconsidered." *Audience Studies Reader.* Ed. Will Brooker and Deborah Jermyn. London: Routledge, 2003. 50–60.

All Access: Celebrity Sibling Showdown. 6 Apr. 2004. <http://www.vh1.com/shows/dyn/vh1_all_access/75181/episode_about.jhtml>.

American Express Blue Cash. Advertisement. *Essence* Apr. 2004: 99.

Animal. Advertisement. *Muscular Development* May 2004: 15–16.

"Annual Awards Special." *PSM* 81 (Feb. 2004): 44–50.

Argyle, Michael. *The Psychology of Social Class.* London: Routledge, 1994.

Aronowitz, Stanley. *How Class Works: Power and Social Movement.* New Haven, CT: Yale UP, 2003.

———. *The Politics of Identity: Class, Culture, Social Movements.* New York: Routledge, 1992.

Atkins Diet Program. Advertisement. *New Yorker* 16–23 Feb. 2004: 95–96.

Auster, Al, and Leonard Quart. "The Working Class Goes to Hollywood." *Cineaste* 9 (1978): 4–7.

Bachman, Gregg, and Thomas J. Slater, eds. *American Silent Film: Discovering Marginalized Voices.* Carbondale: Southern Illinois UP, 2002.

Balibar, Etienne. *Masses, Classes, Ideas: Studies on Politics and Philosophy before and after Marx.* Trans. James Swenson. New York: Routledge, 1994.

———. *On the Dictatorship of the Proletariat.* Trans. Grahame Lock. Surrey, Eng.: Unwin, 1977.

Bank of America. Advertisement. *New Yorker* 16–23 Feb. 2004: 8–9.

Barbas, Samantha. *Movie Crazy: Fans, Stars, and the Cult of Celebrity.* New York: Palgrave, 2001.

Basinger, Jeanine. *A Woman's View: How Hollywood Spoke to Women 1930–1960*. New York: Knopf, 1993.

Baxter, John. *Hollywood in the Thirties*. New York: Paperback Library, 1970.

Beach, Christopher. *Class, Language and American Film Comedy*. Cambridge, Eng.: Cambridge UP, 2002.

Beaudry Diamonds. Advertisement. *Robb Report* Feb. 2004: 10–11.

Benton, Sam, and Reuben Cohen. *Shooting People: Adventures in Reality TV*. London: Verso, 2003.

Black Radiance. Advertisement. *Essence* Apr. 2004: 63.

Bodnar, John. *Blue Collar Hollywood: Liberalism, Democracy, and Working People in American Film*. Baltimore, MD: Johns Hopkins UP, 2003.

Boozer, Jack. *Career Movies: American Business and the Success Mystique*. Austin: U of Texas P, 2002.

Bourdieu, Pierre. *Distinction: A Social Critique of the Judgment of Taste*. Trans. Richard Nice. Cambridge, MA: Harvard UP, 1984.

Breakdown. Advertisement. *Electronic Gaming Monthly* 177 (Apr. 2004): 10–11.

Brooker, Will, and Deborah Jermyn, eds. *Audience Studies Reader*. London: Routledge, 2003.

Brooks, David. *Bobos in Paradise: The New Upper Class and How They Got There*. New York: Simon and Schuster, 2000.

Brottman, Mikita. Introduction. *Car Crash Culture*. Ed. Mikita Brottman. New York: Palgrave, 2001. xi–xli.

Brown, Jamie Foster. "One on One with Serena Williams." *Sister 2 Sister* Apr. 2004: 68–77.

Bryant, Patrick. "Goblin Commander: Unleash the Horde: Smashing Things Is Fun!" *Polygon* 9 (4 Mar. 2004): 50.

Bucholtz, Mary. "From Mulatta to Mestiza: Passing and the Linguistic Reshaping of Ethnic Identity." *Gender Articulated: Language and the Socially Constructed Self*. Ed. Kira Hall and Mary Bucholtz. New York: Routledge, 1995. 351–73.

Butler, Judith. *Gender Trouble: Feminism and the Subversion of Identity*. New York: Routledge, 1999.

Byrnes, Paul V. "*Unreal II*: The Awakening, Good Morning Starshine. The Gun Says, 'Kaboom.'" *Electronic Gaming Monthly* 177 (Apr. 2004): 84–85.

Ca'd'Oro. Advertisement. *Robb Report* Feb. 2004: 101.

"Call of Duty: Finest Hour." *Electronic Gaming Monthly* 177 (Apr. 2004): 102.

"Career CPR." *YM* Apr. 2004: 82.

"Celebrity Cellulite Exposed! How the Stars Try to Cover It Up and How You Can Beat It." *National Enquirer* 8 Mar. 2004: 64–67.

"Celebrity-Inspired Makeover." *Essence* Apr. 2004: 86.

Chou, Che. "Back to Black: Tom Clancy's *Splinter Cell: Pandora Tomorrow.*"
    Xbox Nation Apr. 2004: 74–81.

Clarke, John, Chas Critcher, and Richard Johnson, eds. *Working Class
    Culture.* New York: St. Martin's, 1979.

Cohiba Cigars. Advertisement. *Robb Report* Feb. 2004: 6–7.

Connolly, William E. *Identity Difference: Democratic Negotiations of Political
    Paradox.* Ithaca, NY: Cornell UP, 1991.

Coward, Rosalind. "Class Culture and the Social Formation." *Screen* 18
    (Spring 1977): 75–105.

Daly, Steven. "The Early Years." *Rolling Stone* Special Collectors Issue
    Britney Apr. 2004: 48–60. Reprinted from "Inside the Heart and Mind
    of America's New Teen Queen." *Rolling Stone* 15 Apr. 1999.

Davis, Mike. *Prisoners of the American Dream: Politics and Economy in the
    History of the U.S. Working Class.* London: Verso, 1986.

Dean, Paul. "Bentley Continental GT." *Robb Report* Feb. 2004: 62–64.

Deleuze, Gilles, and Félix Guattari. *Anti-Oedipus: Capitalism and Schizophre-
    nia.* Trans. Robert Hurley, Mark Seem, and Helen R. Lane. Minneapolis:
    U of Minnesota P, 1983.

Dika, Vera. *Recycled Culture in Contemporary Art and Film.* Cambridge,
    Eng.: Cambridge UP, 2003.

Dodge Charger Daytona. Advertisement. *Robb Report Collection* 3 Feb. 2004:
    18–19.

Doherty, Thomas. *Pre-Code Hollywood: Sex, Immorality, and the Insurrection
    in American Cinema 1930–1934.* New York: Columbia UP, 1999.

Dove Milk Promises. Advertisement. *New Yorker* 16–23 Feb. 2004: 209.

Duke, Kacy. "Healthy Body." *Essence* Apr. 2004: 64.

Dyer, Richard. *White.* London: Routledge, 1997.

EAA Corporation for Witness P Carry. Advertisement. *Guns Magazine* May
    2004: 17.

Eckert, Charles. "The Anatomy of a Proletarian Film: Warner's *Marked
    Woman.*" *Imitations of Life: A Reader on Film and Television Melodrama.*
    Ed. Marcia Landy. Detroit: Wayne State UP, 1991. 205–26.

Endless Pool. Advertisement. *Men's Edge* Apr. 2004: 49.

Epstein, Joseph. *Snobbery: The American Version.* Boston: Houghton Mifflin,
    2002.

Exclusive Resorts. Advertisement. *Robb Report* Feb. 2004: 4–5.

"*Extreme Makeover.*" *Reality TV: Official Collector's Edition* Apr. 2004:
    130–33.

Extreme Makeover Web site. 5 Apr. 2004. <http://abc.go.com/primetime/
    extrememakeover/show.html>.

Fahey, Damien. "What I Was Like in High School." *YM* Apr. 2004: 154.

Fedida, Cindy. "Star Treatments." *YM* Apr. 2004: 34.

Felski, Rita. "Nothing to Declare: Identity, Shame, and the Lower Middle Class." *PMLA* 115 (2000): 33–45.

Ferruva, David. "We've All Gone Insane." *Jane* Apr. 2004: 128–31.

Fight Night 2004. Advertisement. *Electronic Gaming Monthly* 177 (Apr. 2004): 6–7.

"Find Your Ideal Weight." *Glamour* Mar. 2004: 141.

Fisher, Jay. "The World Summit for Thermionic Extremism." *Robb Report Collection* Feb. 2004: 51–52.

"Flesh Survey." *Jane* Apr. 2004: 20–23.

Foster, Gwendolyn Audrey. *Performing Whiteness: Postmodern Re/Constructions in the Cinema*. Albany: State U of New York P, 2003.

———. *Troping the Body: Gender, Etiquette, and Performance*. Carbondale: Southern Illinois UP, 2000.

Frank, Thomas. "Lie Down for America: How the Republican Party Sows Ruin on the Great Plains." *Harper's* Apr. 2004: 33–46.

Fremantle Media for the *American Idol* Collectible Card Game. Advertisement. *YM* Apr. 2004: 129.

Friedman, Lester D., ed. *Unspeakable Images: Ethnicity and the American Cinema*. Chicago: U of Illinois P, 1991.

Full Impact Bolt. Advertisement. *Muscular Development* May 2004: 286–87.

Full Spectrum Warrior. *Xbox Nation* Apr. 2004: 56–57.

Fussell, Paul. *Class: A Guide through the American Status System*. New York: Touchstone, 1992.

Giddens, Anthony. *Modernity and Self-Identity: Self and Society in the Late Modern Age*. Stanford, CA: Stanford UP, 1991.

"Girl's Guide to Becoming a Lady, A." *YM* Apr. 2004: 104–9.

Gledhill, Christine, ed. *Home Is Where the Heart Is: Studies in Melodrama and the Woman's Film*. London: BFI, 1987.

Green, Roedy. "What Are Gays Asking For?" 28 Feb. 2004. *Gay and Black Glossary* at <http://mindprod.com/ggloss/gaymarriage.html>. 7 Mar. 2004.

Hall, John R., ed. *Reworking Class*. Ithaca, NY: Cornell UP, 1997.

Halliburton, Karen. "Who Does She Think She Is? She's Christina Norman." *Sister 2 Sister* Apr. 2004: 28–31.

Hansen, Miriam. "Early Silent Cinema: Whose Public Sphere?" *New German Critique* 29 (Spring-Summer 1983): 147–84.

Harris, Bev, with David Allen. *Black Box Voting: Ballot Tampering in the 21st Century*. High Point, NC: Plan Nine, 2003.

Harris, Ron. "Razor Ripped Abs." *Muscular Development* May 2004: 212–29.

Harvey, James. *Romantic Comedy in Hollywood: From Lubitsch to Sturges*. New York: DaCapo, 1998.

Hebdige, Dick. *Subculture: The Meaning of Style*. London: Methuen, 1979.

Heffernan, Virginia. "The Real Boss of 'The Sopranos': Why David Chase Will Never Work in TV Again." *New York Times* 29 Feb. 2004, sect. 2: 1, 20.

Higham, Charles, and Joel Greenberg. *Hollywood in the Forties*. New York: Paperback Library, 1970.

Holland America Line. Advertisement. *New Yorker*. 16–23 Feb. 2004: 14–17.

hooks, bell. *Where We Stand: Class Matters*. New York: Routledge, 2000.

Hummer. Advertisement. *Robb Report* Feb. 2004: 8–9.

Hunter, William C. *Pep: A Book of Hows Not Whys for Physical and Mental Efficiency*. Chicago: Reilly, 1914.

Infinity Q45. Advertisement. *Robb Report* Feb. 2004: 1.

Israel, Betsy. *Bachelor Girl: The Secret History of Single Women in the Twentieth Century*. New York: HarperCollins, 2002.

I Want a Famous Face. <http://www.mtv.com/onair/i_want_a_famous_face/>. 5 Apr. 2004.

I Want a Famous Face—Meet the Patients. <http://www.mtv.com/onair/ i_want_a_famous_face/meet_the_patients/index.jhtml?Patients=Mia>. 5 Apr. 2004.

Jacobs, Lea. "Censorship and the Fallen Woman Cycle." *Home Is Where the Heart Is: Studies in Melodrama and the Woman's Film*. Ed. Christine Gledhill. London: BFI, 1987. 100–12.

James, David. "Is There a Class in This Text? The Repression of Class in Film and Cultural Studies." *A Companion to Film Theory*. Ed. Toby Miller and Robert Stam. Oxford, Eng.: Blackwell, 2004. 182–201.

Jane. Advertisement. *Jane* Apr. 2004: 69.

Jenkins, Henry. "The Work of Theory in the Age of Digital Transformation." *A Companion to Film Theory*. Ed. Toby Miller and Robert Stam. Oxford, Eng.: Blackwell, 2004. 234–61.

Kay, Elsa. "No Excuses: Finding Your Inner Coach." *Men's Edge* Apr. 2004: 38–41.

Khan, Kim. "How Does Your Debt Compare?" *MSN Money*, <http://money-central.msn.com/content/SavingandDebt/P70581.asp?special=0401debt>. 7 Mar. 2004.

King, Geoff. *Film Comedy*. London: Wallflower, 2002.

King, Neal. *Heroes in Hard Times: Cop Action Movies in the U.S.* Philadelphia: Temple UP, 1999.

Kleinhans, Chuck. "Notes on Melodrama and the Family under Capitalism." *Imitations of Life: A Reader on Film and Television Melodrama*. Ed. Marcia Landy. Detroit: Wayne State UP, 1991. 197–204.

Kroeger, Brooke. *Passing: When People Can't Be Who They Are*. New York: Public Affairs, 2003.

Landay, Lori. *Madcaps, Screwballs and Con Women: The Female Trickster in American Culture*. Philadelphia: U of Pennsylvania P, 1998.

Land Rover. Advertisement. *Robb Report* Feb. 2004: 17.

Landy, Marcia, ed. *Imitations of Life: A Reader on Film and Television Melodrama*. Detroit: Wayne State UP, 1991.

LaSalle, Mick. *Dangerous Men: Pre-Code Hollywood and the Birth of the Modern Man.* New York: St. Martin's, 2002.

"Last Minute Diet Secrets." *People* 15 Mar. 2004: 122–23.

Levy, Emanuel. *Small-Town America in Film: The Decline and Fall of Community.* New York: Continuum, 1991.

Lewis, Wyndham. *The Art of Being Ruled.* 1926. Santa Rose: Black Sparrow P, 1989.

Louvish, Simon. *Stan and Ollie: The Roots of Comedy. The Double Life of Laurel and Hardy.* London: Faber and Faber, 2001.

Lynch, Jason, et al. "Class Act." *People* 8 Mar. 2004: 46–51.

Mandel, Ernest. *Power and Money: A Marxist Theory of Bureaucracy.* London: Verso, 1992.

Marshall, Gordon. *Repositioning Class: Social Inequality in Industrial Societies.* London: Sage, 1997.

"Mary J. Blige." *Essence* Apr. 2004: 62.

Matt, Susan J. *Keeping Up with the Joneses: Envy in American Consumer Society, 1890–1930.* Philadelphia: U of Pennsylvania P, 2003.

Mayne, Judith. "Immigrants and Spectators." *Wide Angle* 5 (Fall 1982): 32–41.

McCarthy, Sheryl. "Arrogance Cooked Martha's Goose." Newsday.com, <http://www.newsday.com/news/local/newyork/columnists/ny-vpmcc073697561mar07,0,4204830.column?coll=ny-columnists>. 7 Mar. 2004.

"Men of Valor: Do I Have to Go Back to This Hell Again? (Yes.)" *Xbox Nation* Apr. 2004: 65.

Men's Wearhouse. Advertisement. *Modern Bride* Apr.–May 2004: 103.

Michael Jordan's Senior Flight School. Advertisement. *Robb Report Collection* Feb. 2004: 54.

Munro, Donald, John F. Schumaker, and Stuart C. Carr, eds. *Motivation and Culture.* New York: Routledge, 1997.

Muscio, Giuliana. *Hollywood's New Deal.* Philadelphia: Temple UP, 1997.

Muscular Development. Advertisement. *Muscular Development* May 2004: 418–19.

Newman, Katherine S. *Falling from Grace: The Experience of Downward Mobility in the American Middle Class.* London: Macmillan, 1988.

"New School: Fifty Games You Need to Know About." *Electronic Gaming Monthly* 177 (Apr. 2004): 83–112.

"No Crazy Fan." Letters to the Editor. *Sister 2 Sister* 2004: 88–95.

Off Cycle. Advertisement. *Muscular Development* May 2004: 21–22.

Old Navy. Advertisement for *American Idol.* YM Apr. 2004: 47.

O'Mahoney, Mike. Introduction. *Art Deco.* By Iain Zaczek. Bath, Eng.: Parragon, 2000. 6–15.

Onion, Rebecca. "New VJ on the Block." *YM* Apr. 2004: 82.

Palumbo, Dave. "The Anabolic Freak." *Muscular Development* May 2004: 288–91.

Peretti, Jacques. "You Are a Bad Man Trying to Do Bad Things to Vincent." *Guardian Unlimited* 14 Nov. 2003. <http://film.guardian.co.uk/features/featurepages/0,4120,1084253,00.html>. 7 Mar. 2004.

Perrucci, Robert, and Earl Wysong. *The New Class Society.* New York: Rowman and Littlefield, 1999.

Pfeiffer, Kathleen. *Race Passing and American Individualism.* Boston: U of Massachusetts P, 2003.

Post, Emily. *Etiquette: The Blue Book of Social Usage.* New York: Funk and Wagnalls, 1945.

Prada. Advertisement. *New Yorker* 16–23 Feb. 2004: 12.

Prose, Francine. "Voting Democracy Off the Island: Reality TV and the Republican Ethos." *Harper's* Mar. 2004: 58–64.

Putnam, Carrie Ann. "$25,000 for an 'Average' American Wedding Debunked." Ultimatewedding.com at <http://www.ultimatewedding.com/articles/get.php?action=getarticle&articleid+1164>. 8 Mar. 2004.

Quart, Alissa. *Branded: The Buying and Selling of Teenagers.* Cambridge, MA: Perseus, 2003.

Quddus. "Guest Editor Obsessions, What We're Wasting too Much Time Talking about This Month." *YM* Apr. 2004: 80.

Quotations Page, The. <http://www.quotationspage.com/quotes/Andy_Warhol>. 5 Apr. 2004.

Ratledge, Ingela. "The *Us* Buzz-o-Meter." *US Weekly* 1 Mar. 2004: 34.

"Red Carpet." *Rolling Stone* Special Collectors Issue *Britney Spears* Apr. 2004: 12–17.

Redemption. Advertisement. *Essence* Apr. 2004: 145.

Redemption. The Movie Insider. <http://movies.themovieinsider.com/?mid=1503>. 1 Apr. 2004.

Roffman, Peter, and Jim Purdy. "The Worker and Hollywood." *Cineaste* 9 (1978): 8–13.

Romano, John. "The War on Weapons of Mass Construction: Bush Says No Roids. Now What?" *Muscular Development* May 2004: 238–45.

Ross, Robert. "Car of the Year 2004." *Robb Robert* Feb. 2004: 60–95.

Ross, Steven J. *Working-Class Hollywood: Silent Film and the Shaping of Class in America.* Princeton, NJ: Princeton UP, 1998.

Rubin, Gayle. "The Traffic in Women: Notes on the 'Political Economy' of Sex." *Women, Class, and the Feminist Imagination: A Socialist Feminist Reader.* Ed. Karen V. Hansen and Ilene J. Philipson. Philadelphia: Temple UP, 1990: 74–113.

"Runway Report." *Modern Bride* Apr.–May 2004: 370–81.

Russell Athletic. Advertisement. *Men's Health* Apr. 2004: 55.

Ryan, Jake, and Charles Sackrey. *Strangers in Paradise: Academics from the Working Class.* Boston: South End P, 1984.

Ryan, Michael, and Douglas Kellner. *Camera Politica: The Politics and Ideology of Contemporary Hollywood Film.* Bloomington: Indiana UP, 1988.

Sánchez, María Carla, and Linda Schlossberg, eds. *Passing; Identity and Interpretation in Sexuality, Race and Religion.* New York: New York UP, 2000.

Schor, Juliet B. *The Overspent American: Upscaling, Downshifting, and the New Consumer.* New York: Basic Books, 1998.

Seem, Mark. Introduction. *Anti-Oedipus: Capitalism and Schizophrenia.* By Gilles Deleuze and Félix Guattari. 1977. Minneapolis: U of Minnesota P, 1983. xv–xxiv.

Sennett, Richard, and Jonathan Cobb. *The Hidden Injuries of Class.* 1966. New York: Norton, 1993.

Scott Kay Platinum Jewelers. Advertisement. *Modern Bride* Apr.–May 2004: 2–3.

Shapouri, Beth. "Class vs. Crass." *YM* Apr. 2004: 32.

Shaviro, Steven. *The Cinematic Body.* Minneapolis: U of Minnesota P, 1993.

Shnayerson, Michael. "Hack the Vote." *Vanity Fair* Apr. 2004: 158–80.

Simon, G., et al. Advertisement. *Modern Bride.* Apr.–May 2004: 369.

Situationist International Collective. "On the Poverty of Student Life." *Situationist International Anthology.* Ed. and trans. Ken Knabb. 1966. Berkeley, CA: Bureau of Public Secrets, 1981. 319–37.

Slits, The. *Cut.* Virgin, 1979.

Smith, Charles Merrill. *Instant Status: Or How to Become a Pillar of the Upper Middle Class.* New York: Doubleday, 1972.

Somers, Margaret R. "The Narrative Construction of Identity: A Relational and Network Approach." *Theory and Society* 23 (1994): 605–49.

"So Real—In Touch with Their Real Sides!" *In Touch Weekly* 1 Mar. 2004: 92–93.

Splinter Cell, Rainbow Six 3, and Ghost Recon: Jungle Storm. Advertisement. *Electronic Gaming Monthly* 177 (Apr. 2004): 70–82.

SportsArt 807 Elliptical. Advertisement. *Men's Edge* Apr. 2004: 41.

Stabile, Carol A., ed. *Turning the Century: Essays in Media and Cultural Studies.* Oxford: Westview, 2000.

Stamp, Shelley. *Movie-Struck Girls: Woman and Motion Picture Culture after the Nickelodeon.* Princeton, NJ: Princeton UP, 2000.

Stylander, Stephanie Pfreinder. "The Price Is Right." *Modern Bride* Apr.–May 2004: 344–53.

Tasker, Yvonne. *Working Girls: Gender and Sexuality in Popular Culture.* London: Routledge, 1998.

Taylor, John Russell. *Strangers in Paradise: The Hollywood Emigrés 1933–1950.* London: Faber and Faber, 1983.

Tenth Victim, The. Amazon.com. <http://www.amazon.com/exec/obidos/ASIN/6305840091/ref=ase_imdb-adbox/002-3348613-2197657>. 5 Apr. 2004.

Thompson, Michael. "Kate's Body." *Jane* Apr. 2004: 110–13.

Titus, Craig. "Titus Talks." *Muscular Development* May 2004: 370, 372.

Tomczak, Sarah. "Stars—They're Just Like Us." *US Weekly* 1 Mar. 2004: 24–25.

Toulet, Emmanuelle. *Birth of the Motion Picture.* Trans. Susan Emanuel. New York: Abrams, 1995.

Traube, Elizabeth G. *Class, Gender, and Generation in 1980s Hollywood Movies.* San Francisco: Westview, 1992.

Turner, Niki. "Happy Number 3, Avant." *Sister 2 Sister* Apr. 2004: 42–49.

United States Virgin Islands. Advertisement. *Essence* Apr. 2004: 191.

Urciuoli, Bonnie. "Representing Class: Who Decides?" *Anthropological Quarterly* 66 (Oct. 1993): 203–10.

Veblen, Thorstein. *The Theory of the Leisure Class.* New York: Dover, 1994.

Viviani, Christian. "Who Is Without Sin? The Maternal Melodrama in American Film, 1930–39." *Home Is Where the Heart Is: Studies in Melodrama and the Woman's Film.* Ed. Christine Gledhill. London: BFI, 1987. 83–99.

V12 Turbo. Advertisement. *Muscular Development* May 2004: 40–41.

Wald, Gayle. *Crossing the Line: Racial Passing in Twentieth Century U.S. Literature and Culture.* Durham, NC: Duke UP, 2000.

Weathers, Diane. "Straight Talk: Living Paycheck to Paycheck?" *Essence* Apr. 2004: 30.

Westime. Advertisement. *Robb Report* Feb. 2004: 2–3.

Wheeler, Flex. "West Coast Warriors." *Muscular Development* May 2004: 174–91.

"Where Are They Now?" *TV Guide* 3–10 Apr. 2004: 32–42.

Wild, Paul. "Recreation in Rochdale, 1900–40." *Working Class Culture.* Ed. John Clarke, Chas Critcher, and Richard Johnson. New York: St. Martin's, 1979: 140–60.

Williams, Linda. "'Something Else Besides a Mother': *Stella Dallas* and the Maternal Melodrama." *Imitations of Life: A Reader on Film and Television Melodrama.* Ed. Marcia Landy. Detroit: Wayne State UP, 1991. 307–30.

Wilson, Stevie. "Shaving Off Time." *Men's Edge* Apr. 2004: 26–30.

Wray, Matt, and Annalee Newitz, eds. *White Trash: Race and Class in America.* New York: Routledge, 1997.

Wright, Erik Olin. *Classes.* London: Verso, 1985.

X-Ray Spex. *Germfree Adolescents.* Mobjack, 1978.

Xvest. Advertisement. *Men's Edge* Apr. 2004: 63.

Index

Gwendolyn Audrey Foster is a professor of film studies, women's studies, and cultural studies in the Department of English at the University of Nebraska, Lincoln. Her most recent book, *Performing Whiteness: Postmodern Re/Constructions in the Cinema,* was named an outstanding title in the humanities for 2004 by *Choice.* Her other books include *Captive Bodies: Postcolonial Subjectivity in Cinema, Troping the Body,* and *Identity and Memory: The Films of Chantal Akerman.* She also coedits the journal *Quarterly Review of Film and Video.*